THE WORD MADE PLAIN

THE WORD MADE PLAIN

The Power and Promise of Preaching

Harold Solomon,
Stay in the Word!
Thanks!

JAMES HENRY HARRIS

Jonnyac̄
3/05

Fortress Press
Minneapolis

Scripture quotations are the author's own unless otherwise noted. Those from the New Revised Standard Version Bible (NRSV) are copyright © 1989 by the Division of Christian Education of the National Council of the Churches of Christ in the USA and are used by permission. Those from *The New English Bible* (NEB) are copyright © 1961, 1970 by the Delegates of the Oxford University Press and the Syndics of the Cambridge University Press and are reprinted by permission. Those from the *Good News Bible* (TEV) are copyright © 1966, 1971, 1976 by the American Bible Society and are used by permission.

"Prayer" in chapter 4 is from *Selected Poems of Langston Hughes*, copyright © 1927 by Alfred A. Knopf, Inc. and renewed 1955 by Langston Hughes. Used by permission of Alfred A. Knopf, a division of Random House, Inc. and Harold Ober Associates.

"Listen, Lord—A Prayer" and "Preface" in chapter 5 are from *God's Trombones* by James Weldon Johnson, copyright © 1927 The Viking Press, Inc., renewed © 1955 by Grace Nail Johnson. Used by permission of Viking Penguin, a division of Penguin Group (USA) Inc.

Cover design: James Korsmo
Interior design: Zan Ceeley

Library of Congress Cataloging-in-Publication Data

Harris, James H.
  The Word made plain : the power and promise of preaching / James Henry Harris.
    p. cm.
  Includes bibliographical references and index.
  ISBN 0-8006-3687-2 (alk. paper)
  1. African American preaching. I. Title.
  BV4208.U6H375 2004
  251'.0089'96073—dc22

                      2004010621

To three similar and yet uniquely different princes
of the African American pulpit

John Malcus Ellison (1889–1979)

Samuel DeWitt Proctor (1921–1997)

Miles Jerome Jones (1925–2002)

And to my parents (deceased)

[John] Richard and Carrie Anna Jones Harris

Contents

Preface

When the preacher in the Black church preaches the gospel, it is not unusual for persons from the pews to encourage the preacher dialogically by saying, "Make it plain, preacher," or "That's right, make it clear, work it out, make it plain now." I have always interpreted these words to mean that there is a definite conversation going on between the preacher and the hearer. And inherent in this dialogue is the assertion by the hearer that the preacher is in fact on target, clarifying the Word of God. This means that the statement "make it plain" is a phrase in praise of the sermon and the effectiveness of the preacher. This statement, when translated from the language of the African American church, means that "you are doing alright, preacher" or "stay the course" or "keep preaching the way you are preaching." To make the Word plain is to interpret the Word in a way that speaks to the heart and soul of the parishioner. It means to interpret the biblical text and the congregation's context in a way that helps them to understand how to cope with the difficulties and joys of life. Making it plain means making it real, boldly proclaiming the Word of God to the oppressed and the oppressors, to those within and without the walls of the church. The Word made plain is the power of the gospel in this day and time. It is daring to declare "thus saith the Lord!" in the spirit of the prophets like Jeremiah, Amos, and Martin Luther King Jr.

This book is for preachers, pastors, and other students of preaching in any tradition and provides them an opportunity to learn from the African American preaching tradition and its intersections with other traditions. This book reflects a host of perspectives, from those of Martin Luther King Jr. to recent philosophical and theological thinkers. Other voices can be heard as well, including the powerful voices of John Malcus Ellison, Samuel DeWitt Proctor, and Miles Jerome Jones. These three kings of educational excellence, princes of the pulpit, and pastors in the African American church are also the voices of transformation and hope, voices of reason and rhetorical genius. They illumine the principles I discuss as keys to powerful preaching.

Since in this book I advocate the style and substance of Black preaching to all Christian preachers, a word about the context of the Black church is in order. In spite of their acculturation and adaptation to much of what exists in the larger society, the Black church and Black religion remain the paradigmatic embodiment of the cultural life of African Americans. The Black church represents freedom and independence more clearly than any other institution with which Blacks are associated. It is the only American institution that is owned, operated, and controlled by Blacks. Nothing else in Black life is as ubiquitous as the Black church and the Black preacher. Even persons who are not Christian or even religious participate in the social life of the Black church. The Black church often seems to be as much a social and political entity as it is a religious one.

History lives on in the Black church that directly affects preaching. The relationship between slavery, religion, and skin color permeates the history of Blacks in the United States. In turn, one's blackness forever affects any lived understanding of philosophy, theology, ethics, and social reality. After being stolen from their homeland and sold into slavery, and after hundreds of years of chattel slavery, Blacks continue to suffer from the vestiges of segregation and racial hatred that have characterized American history from Columbus's "discovery" to the present. Black people have inherited a legacy of injustice, domination, hatred, and discrimination that defies the Constitution and any other documents that pronounce all people to be equal and entitled to liberty and justice.

The Black church is a socially diverse, sociologically and theologically complicated phenomenon. Yet seven major denominations comprise 80 to 85 percent of all Blacks who profess to be Christians.[1] The Black church remains overwhelmingly Baptist, African Methodist, and Church of God in Christ.

The Black church is unique in that it was organized and developed by an oppressed group, shut off from the institutional life of the larger society. During and after slavery, this invisible, often clandestine convocation of believers used their church and religion as a way of coping with the realities of injustice, discrimination, and racism manifested in customs and laws. As a result of society denying Blacks the institutional access and outlets necessary for normal social existence, the Black church became a vehicle for the pursuit of freedom, justice, and equality in society at large.[2]

It is this heritage of justice, of moral suasion, of coming to terms with the realities of race, and of cultural critique that can be instructive and helpful to all Christian churches in today's context. This role of the Black church affects the way Black preachers read the Word and the way they preach the Word. It has formed the basis for a great tradition of preaching that can enrich homiletics for Christians of any racial or ethnic background. This book is an effort to explain and teach the best of homiletics from the perspective of the Black church. The following chapters outline the hermeneutical roots of Black preaching, highlight a few of its noted practitioners, explain its distinctive interpretive practice, aesthetic dimension, and use of narrative, and lay out the process of sermon development. I exemplify that process with sermons, one of which is included at the end of each chapter. The sermons themselves best demonstrate the homiletical task.

◈◈◈

I am grateful for the opportunity to have had John Malcus Ellison as my catechist for ordination and to have been taught preaching by Samuel DeWitt Proctor and Miles Jerome Jones. In this sense, I am a very blessed and thankful person. While they are not in any way responsible for my weaknesses or shortcomings, I am indebted to them for the little that I know about the practice of preaching and the teaching of this noble craft.

I want to thank the following persons for their assistance with this manuscript: Professors Ronald Allen and Cleo LaRue were the first to read the entire manuscript and offered valuable advice as to how it could be improved. Tom Long, James Nieman, and Paul Scott Wilson were very helpful in their reading of the manuscript. Each provided insightful comments that have been used to make the book clearer. Several of the chapters were first developed in seminars at the University of Virginia, where I have been a community scholar for the past several years doing postdoctoral study in theology, ethics, and culture. I have been privileged to have professors John Milbank, Charles Marsh, Larry Bouchard, and Charles Mathewes offer their critique of several of these chapters when they were in the developmental stage and/or to contribute to my understanding of philosophical theology, ethics, and religion and culture. Moreover, several of these chapters were first presented at the annual meetings of the Academy of Homiletics. I have benefited from their discussions and the suggestions of several participants in the theology and preaching, preaching and worship, and hermeneutics and Bible work groups. I owe much gratitude and thanks to the distinguished professor Gayraud Wilmore, who consented to read the manuscript in spite of his busy schedule and other commitments. To the editors at Fortress Press, I am always grateful: J. Michael West, Ron Bonner, Marshall Johnson, Zan Ceeley, and Karen Schenkenfelder.

The following persons served as research assistants for several sections of this project: the Rev. Audrey Thompson and the Rev. Kenneth Gates, who provided valuable information from their class notes on Miles Jones and the archives at Virginia Union's library on John M. Ellison. Information on Samuel D. Proctor came from his books and tapes of his sermons as well as my own class notes when I was a doctoral student in homiletics with him at United Theological Seminary. I am indebted to Boykin Sanders, New Testament professor at Virginia Union, for his insight in helping to clarify the meaning of texts and the language of story in African American preaching.

Also, the late Miles Jerome Jones, who was our senior professor of preaching at Virginia Union until his death in December 2002, read several sections and offered very helpful suggestions. I am always grateful for his wisdom and willingness to help the preacher. He was pleased when I became pastor of Second Baptist Church, and he remained a confidante and encourager until his death. He would often show up on Sunday mornings to worship with us; however, I always felt some anxiety whenever he was in the audience. This anxiety was due to my own trepidation in the presence of such a powerful spiritual teacher and preacher of the Word.

Also, my colleague Nathan Dell has been a type of preaching coach and has encouraged me in this work. Thanks to the Rev. Raymond Reid, who provided valuable research assistance and information on narrative preaching. The Rev. Kimberly Clark typed the final manuscript and provided valuable assistance in formatting the document. The Rev. Charlotte

McSwine-Harris has been my most dedicated personal assistant for many years and has worked diligently in reading and typing this manuscript from its inception. She has also been a research assistant for this book and others.

Finally, I have presented portions of this manuscript to the students and faculty at the School of Theology at Virginia Union University, especially those in my seminar on the preaching and theology of Martin Luther King Jr., as well as those in the required middler course, Preaching and Worship II, and to our study group, the Dialectical Society.

I am also grateful to our church musicians, James H. Lyle and Anne H. Williams, both master musicians, for their research assistance in locating the words of the Negro spiritual "I Heard the Preaching of the Elder" or "I Heard de Preachin' of de Word o' God." Also, Larry Seilhamer, Public Services Librarian, Saint Paul's College, Lawrenceville, Virginia, has helped to track down sources during the final stage of editing this book. While I have been helped by many, I am solely responsible for any shortcomings of this book.

As always, I am thankful to the Second Baptist Church Congregation and last but not least to my wife, Demetrius, and my sons, James Corey and Cameron Christopher, for their unending support and encouragement during the many phases of my ministry, including the writing of this book. Without their support, my ministry, teaching, and preaching would be an almost impossible task.

1

The Preacher's Self-Understanding

Know thyself.
—Socrates

A believing way of knowing means to know oneself overcome
and pardoned by the person of Christ in the preached word.
—Dietrich Bonhoeffer, *Act and Being*

Then something happened, something that has changed and
transformed my life to the present day . . . and in particular
the Sermon on the Mount freed me. . . . It was a great liberation. It became clear to me that the life of a servant of Jesus
Christ must belong to the church, and step by step it became
plainer to me how far that must go.
—Eberhard Bethge, *Dietrich Bonhoeffer*

At that moment I experienced the presence of the Divine as I
had never before experienced him. It seemed as though I could
hear the quiet assurance of an inner voice saying, "Stand up
for righteousness, stand up for truth. God will be at your side
forever."
—Martin Luther King Jr., *Strength to Love*

To preach the gospel effectively, the preacher must seek self-
understanding on a continuing basis. Each person who
aspires to preach must come to grips with the frailties and
faults of the self—the earthen vessels in which the gospel treas-

ure is delivered to the congregation. This is the challenge and the joy, the burden and the blessing of preaching.

Self-understanding is a difficult phenomenon because as a rule, we tend to concentrate on the "other" both in our judging and in our analysis. This means that we do not perceive the otherness in our own self but see the self as distinct and different from the other. Jesus was keenly aware of this in his indictments against the Pharisees, saying they could see the speck in someone else's eye but not the log in their own (Matthew 7:5). Similarly, Paul encourages his hearers in Corinth to examine themselves before engaging in the Lord's Supper: "Examine yourselves, and only then eat of the bread and drink of the cup" (1 Corinthians 11:28, NRSV). Self-examination is critical in our struggle toward wholeness and self-actualization, and self-understanding is a necessary precondition to doing ministry effectively.

The renowned psychiatrist Carl Jung points out that "we know how to distinguish ourselves from other animals in point of anatomy and physiology, but as conscious, reflecting beings gifted with speech, we lack all criteria for self-judgment."[1] In these times, when the church and world seem to be suffering from moral decay and economic injustice, we are compelled to look at ourselves in a more holistic and self-critical way. Self-examination is a look into our own being, context, and character in an effort to assess critically the nature of self. It is the process of understanding the inner recesses of our lives with a sense of openness and truth. Quite frankly, our selves need to be purged! The psalmist, while praying for moral renewal, makes this clearer when he writes, "You desire truth in the inward being; therefore teach me wisdom in my secret heart. Purge me with hyssop, and I shall be clean" (Psalm 51:6–7a, NRSV).

We have to reach the point of seeing ourselves for who we really are; then and only then can a change take place in our lives. Too many of us resist the power of internal and external change simply because our experiences have been so limited that we are unable to cope with new ideas and new ways of life. But change and growth are not static phenomena. They are achieved through self-understanding.

The Black Church and Self-Understanding

In ways both spiritual and practical, the church contributes to self-understanding. The church helps to form the social world of its participants. In activities and worship, persons come together to relate, reflect, and review each other's behaviors and practices. In business meetings, fellowship dinners, and choir rehearsals, people struggle to understand themselves and their cohorts. They try to be themselves, to free themselves from oppression and injustice, from guilt and pain, from fear and doubt. The life of church folk is about the culture of a people, their beliefs, feelings, gestures, expressions, their use and understanding of language, and theology as praxis.

When I first began to serve as pastor, I learned much about Christian ethics and theology from practicing Christians in the local church community. Many of them were marvelous examples of truth, fairness, and justice. They displayed attitudes that showed respect and family solidarity, compassion and kindness, Christian loyalty and devout living. I will forever remember how church officers took me under their wings and nurtured my undeveloped and somewhat embryonic theology and spirituality. This helped my self-understanding and enabled me to minister to them. In the words of folk in the African American church, I have been able to hear the pain and agony, the strength and stamina, the doubt and convictions of those whose lives are a constant struggle of negotiating the tension between good and evil, joy and sorrow. This constant struggle, while not unique to African Americans, is emblematically captured in Black church history.

The dialectic comes through in the voices that are heard—voices that will speak of commitment to Jesus Christ, church, and community on the one hand, and fear, anger, and frustration on the other. These voices have seldom been heard because the world of theologians, philosophers, and pastors is often outside their purview. I have no doubt that they talk to each other, but this talk is usually among themselves, largely ignored by preachers and scholars. Let those who have an ear hear the cries of the people, and let the people's tears contribute to the hearers' self-understanding.

The Selfhood of the Preacher: The Example of Martin Luther King Jr.

Another contributor to my self-understanding has been Martin Luther King Jr. I am deeply indebted to him for his courage and for single-handedly raising the bar for the American preacher. As a man who grew up during the King years, I can identify a connection between my call to the preaching ministry and my admiration of his eloquence. Martin Luther King Jr. has had a significant impact on my own concept of self and my understanding of who I am as a person and a preacher of the gospel of liberation and transformation.

Martin Luther King Jr. was a hybrid, an amalgam of the refinement of his mother, Alberta Parks, and the rugged, sometimes brusque and dogged determination of his father, Martin Luther King Sr. The son was poised and calm in his speech pattern and behavior, but the words he used were often terse and boldly acidic. Although his words had a cutting-edge quality, he would assert that anger over racism and segregation was not enough. One must actually do something about it. In his sermon to the American Baptist Convention on May 30, 1964, King three times used the searing and cutting word *stupid* to refer to men who fostered racism and injustice. This reminds me of the boldness of the prophets Amos and Jeremiah. Additionally, in my view, King possessed a radicality, often masked by his humble personality and mastery of words and language, that lured the most hateful person into his circle of love. By moral suasion, logic, and compelling eloquence, he was able to bring down the strong and defiant walls of segregation. His use of the language of Christian theology and of democracy and freedom, a language employed by the architects of the Constitution and the Declaration of Independence, enabled him to prick the conscience of America and the world.

The face of Martin Luther King Jr. is indeed the face of the prophetic preacher, the face of the Civil Rights Movement, and the face of the oppressed. He represents more than any other—even Rosa Parks, Roy Wilkins, or Thurgood Marshall—the face of Black America in its quest for justice and fairness. It is because of this face and the voice that emanates from it that I identify King as the embodiment of manhood, justice, peace, and love. The face of Martin Luther King Jr. was a source of pride for millions of Black faces throughout the world.

In seeing the face of Dr. Martin Luther King Jr., a person was compelled to feel a sense of dignity and pride that was seldom evoked by other faces. More precisely, this was the experience of seeing one's own face as an African American growing up in the vile and segregated South, a place so hateful and prejudiced that Blacks were forever reminded of their status as second-class citizens by every level of government, local, state, and federal, and by the self-appointed leaders and guardians of the status quo from the Ku Klux Klan and the White Citizens' Councils to the state senators and governors of the southern states.

King's physical face, his external face, was critically important to the self-understanding of a generation of African Americans. This is not to minimize or obviate his inner self, his struggles with being a husband and father, a pastor and community leader. There certainly is an absolute and entangled connection between this external face and the inner workings of the mind and soul. But the image of King's face across television sets and on pages of newspapers and magazines gave me a sense of self-esteem and pride that I to this very day cannot adequately articulate. This sense of being, this ontological "isness" was instilled within millions of African Americans by the powerful image of his Black face. The face alone, devoid of word or deed, helped to give meaning and value to the person of the preacher.

From the face, words are uttered and gestures are expressed. Preaching in his thunderous baritone voice, King demanded that one sit up, pay attention, and take note that something important and prophetic was being said. The face as the "site of human communication," "the locus of speech," is clearly why the face is so important to the preacher.[2] From the preacher's face bursts forth the eruptions of the Holy Spirit, the convictions of the heart, and the concepts and ideas of love and justice. The preacher's concept of self and world is articulated through the voice and expressions of the face.

However, as I have suggested earlier, the face is the most glaring representation of race. The face of a Black man, Martin Luther King Jr., by its very color, its dark shade of brown with commanding lips and strong voice, helped to make his speech, his sermons the embodiment of self-esteem and self-respect. Moreover, his encouragement to Black America to feel good about its heritage, its manhood and womanhood was critical to Black self-understanding. King encouraged African Americans to assert themselves in ways that would foster freedom, dignity, and honor. The spirit of this self-assertion is evident throughout his career, but it culminated on April 3, 1968, when he said in those unforgettable words from Memphis, "I am not fearing any man; mine eyes have seen the glory of the coming of the Lord."

Martin Luther King Jr. on Black Power and Selfhood

Some of King's most profound and enduring words on self and self-esteem emerge from his sustained analysis and critique of Black Power in *Where Do We Go from Here: Chaos or Community?* Black Power seems to represent the dialectical tension that King often struggled with and to some extent reconciled via his love ethic and his hope for integration. He writes:

> Out of the soil of slavery came the psychological roots of the Black Power cry. Anyone familiar with the Black Power movement recognizes that defiance of white authority and white power is a constant theme; the defiance almost becomes a kind of taunt. Underneath it, however, there is a legitimate concern that the Negro break away from "unconditional submission" and thereby assert his own selfhood.[3]

While King was not in agreement with the language of Black Power, he recognized the spirit of the movement and the value it served for the development of the Black self. King acknowledged that this arousing of manhood in a people who had been slaves and been taught systematically that they are "nobody" is difficult.[4] King reiterates the positive elements of Black Power as conveying self-worth:

> One must not overlook the positive value in calling the Negro to a new sense of manhood, to a deep feeling of racial pride and to an audacious appreciation of his heritage. The Negro must be grasped by a new realization of his dignity and worth. He must stand up amid a system that still oppresses him and develop an unassailable and majestic sense of his own value. He must no longer be ashamed of being black.[5]

King clearly empathizes with the philosophical and psycholog-ical foundations of the Black Power movement, and he embod-ied much of what the movement espoused.

Not only was he not ashamed of being Black, but his sear-ing and systematic attack on white racism was designed to cre-ate shame in the minds and hearts of white people. His ability to connect history and theology, word and deed and elo-quently enumerate the unconscionable crimes perpetrated against Blacks shamed the white leaders of a nation that espoused democracy and freedom. Also, King's use of the national news media probably hastened the enactment of some Civil Rights laws. The vivid images of police dogs biting Blacks, policemen on horses whipping and beating Black women, men, and youth, and water hoses turned on old Black men and women sharply contrasted with King in handcuffs, singing freedom songs. This stark contrast created a sense of the reality of injustice, racism, and the effects of segregation that heretofore had not been seen throughout the so-called free world. This American apartheid caused a degree of shame in the hearts of those who couldn't believe that the face of white America on television was represented by Bull Conner, George Wallace, Jim Clarke, and policemen with helmets and billy clubs beating Black God-fearing Christians.

Under these circumstances, every Black American felt ten-sion in the self, and King expressed his understanding of that tension in his difficulty with the use of the term *Black Power*. This language, and the ideology and movement behind it, troubled King, but it also provided the opportunity for him to develop a workable interpretation of the Black self. He recog-nized that deep within the language and spirit of Black Power was the foundational assertion of "somebodiness" that was necessary and healthy for the Black psyche:

The tendency to ignore the Negro's contribution to American life and strip him of his personhood is as old as the earliest history books and as contemporary as the morning's newspaper. To offset this cultural homicide, the Negro must rise up with an affirmation of his own Olympian manhood. Any movement for the Negro's freedom that overlooks this necessity is only waiting to be buried. As long as the mind is enslaved the body can never be free. Psychological freedom, a firm sense of self-esteem, is the most powerful weapon against the long night of physical slavery. No Lincolnian Emancipation Proclamation or Kennedyan or Johnsonian civil rights bill can totally bring this kind of freedom. The Negro will only be truly free when he reaches down to the inner depths of his own being and signs with the pen and ink of assertive selfhood his own emancipation proclamation.[6]

The assertive selfhood that King speaks of was overtly represented by the more radical and younger participants in the civil rights movement, such as Stokely Carmichael. This does not mean, however, that King himself was not assertive; he was absolutely assertive, but his assertive self was tempered by practical reason and augmented by his understanding of the lessons of history. He often warned that the African American could not win a violent and physical revolution, because the will of the people would not support it, nor would the United States armed forces. King was a pragmatist or realist as well as an idealist in the sense that he was able to hang on to the philosophy of nonviolence as a form of resistance even though it often precipitated resistance and violence.

While King argued that ontological freedom was an internal psychological attribute that had to be claimed individually by every African American, he understood that the shackles and

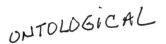
ONTOLOGICAL

chains of legislated segregation were unjust and created a de facto inequality in practical life that was tantamount to unfreedom. This "assertive selfhood" was the only way for the African American to show forth his manhood or her womanhood. In fact, the Civil Rights Movement has its embryonic genesis grounded in the defiant "no" of the assertive self of Rosa Parks. This assertive selfhood was in fact the beginning of the new emancipation proclamation for African Americans nearly one hundred years after Abraham Lincoln.

King continues his discussion of the self and self-esteem by stating:

> With a spirit straining toward true self-esteem, the Negro must boldly throw off the manacles of self-abnegation and say to himself and the world: "I am somebody. I am a person. I am a man with dignity and honor. I have a rich and noble history, however painful and exploited that history has been. I am black *and* comely." This self-affirmation is the black man's need made compelling by the white man's crimes against him. This is positive and necessary power for black people.[7]

This language, which King used in the 1960s, was a forerunner to the speech of Jesse Jackson and other sloganeers. The chant "I am somebody" was later paralleled with "Say it loud, I'm Black and I'm proud" and "Up with hope, down with dope." All of these image-boosting and self-assertive words helped to confer upon the African American a sense of somebodiness that erupted from what King called "the inner depths of his own being."

In spite of King's words and hope, integration as a practical ideal has failed to empower Black people. Black Power—economic justice and the empowerment of oppressed people—is as elusive today as it was thirty years ago. Boykin Sanders is correct when he argues that the desire of Blacks to integrate and occupy spaces previously forbidden because of race has served to define African freedom in America. Just as Rosa Parks said no to segregation on the public buses of Montgomery, Sanders says that "whites in America would say no to Black Power as defined by Black Power advocates and African masses. While civil rights was not a big problem for whites (indeed it increased their economic holdings), Black Power—it seemed to most whites—was."[8]

I propose that King's notion of the self and his insistence on the fact that Black people had within their own being the power to assert themselves psychologically, spiritually, and politically is constitutive of Black Power. It is a Black Power mediated by reason and practicality. This is consistent with King's understanding of the meaning of power and its correlates, love and justice:

> Power, properly understood, is the ability to achieve purpose. It is the strength required to bring about social, political or economic changes. In this sense power is not only desirable but necessary in order to implement the demands of love and justice. One of the greatest problems of history is that the concepts of love and power are usually contrasted as polar opposites. Love is identified with a resignation of power and power with a denial of love. It was this misinterpretation that caused Nietzsche, the philosopher of the 'will to power,' to reject the Christian concept of love. . . . What is needed is a realization that power without love is reckless and abusive and that love without power is sentimental and anemic. Power at its best is love implementing the demands of justice. Justice at its best is love connecting everything that stands against love.[9]

As this passage reveals, King was influenced by Paul Tillich's correlations between love, power, and justice.[10]

The Self and the Church: Martin Luther King Jr. on the White Church

King's most enduring prophetic writing is his "Letter from the Birmingham City Jail." This letter has the tone and prophetic judgment of Amos or Jeremiah. Jewish scholar Abraham Heschel placed King in the lineage of the great Old Testament prophets who espoused justice and righteousness as primary in any normative ethic and theology. In that letter, while King is probably disappointed with both the Black and white churches, he reserves some of his most stinging criticism for the white church and its leadership. He states:

> I must honestly reiterate that I have been disappointed with the church. I do not say that as one of the negative critics who can always find something wrong with the church. I say it as a minister of the gospel, who loves the church; who was nurtured in its bosom; who has been sustained by its spiritual blessings and who will remain true to it as long as the cord of life shall lengthen.[11]

King's disappointment with the church grew out of the painful realization that the white church was intimately connected with the southern power structure of prejudice, segregation, and racism. King had hoped that the white church was a Christian church first and white secondarily; however, he quickly learned differently. His Birmingham experience reinforced this reality that the church was white first and foremost, and any moral courage or Christian principles of love and justice were obviously lacking or secondary to maintaining the status quo. He writes with poignant clarity:

In the midst of blatant injustices inflicted upon the Negro, I have watched white churches stand on the sideline and merely mouth pious irrelevancies and sanctimonious trivialities. In the midst of a mighty struggle to rid our nation of racial and economic injustice, I have heard so many ministers say "Those are social issues with which the gospel has no real concern," and I have watched so many churches commit themselves to a completely otherworldly religion which made a strange distinction between body and soul, the sacred and the secular.[12]

The white church was not interested in lending her voice to the freedom quest of African Americans because it constituted the "principalities and powers" as much as any of the other architects of segregation and institutionalized inequality. This is the same church that for centuries had blatantly practiced discrimination, sanctioned and encouraged slavery, and helped to construct the status quo.

Yet King had an unrealistic hope for the church. He reiterates his disappointment by stating:

I have traveled the length and breath of Alabama, Mississippi and all the other southern states. On sweltering summer days and crisp autumn mornings I have looked at her beautiful churches with their lofty spires pointing heavenward. . . . Over and over again I have found myself asking: "What kind of people worship here? Who is their God?"[13]

The God of the white church has historically been grounded in the status quo, the constitution, and a white-supremacy ideology. This "triune god" enables the white church to be an agent of the government, a harbinger of civil religion, an arm of the republic or the democratic state, and a propagator of the state's values and ideology. The white church seems to be very much in complicity with racism, white supremacy, and a gospel devoid of the focus on Jesus as a radical transformer of culture.

Martin Luther King Jr. viewed the church as the body of Christ. "But, oh! How we have blemished and scarred that body through social neglect and fear of being nonconformists."[14] King often romanticizes the church, glorying in her lofty history and early formations. But the response of the white church was very disappointing, because King was a product of the Black church and somehow naively thought that these two institutions would come together in fighting against racism and injustice. He was sorely mistaken! He concluded that "the contemporary church is often a weak, ineffectual voice with an uncertain sound. It is so often the arch-supporter of the status quo. . . . The power structure of the average community is consoled by the church's silent and often vocal sanction of things as they are."[15] The uncertain sound of the church can be laid directly at the preacher's feet. As preeminent Black preacher Samuel Proctor argues, the sermon be not uncertain, but very certain, as expressed by the title of his book *The Certain Sound of the Trumpet.*

King's indictment of the church is caused by his great love for the church and his understanding of self. His very being was connected with the church. Born into a family of preachers and church folk both paternally and maternally, King could not think of himself or assert himself without the influence of the church. He makes this plain by saying, "Yes, I love the church; I love her sacred walls. How could I do otherwise? I am in the rather unique position of being the son, the grandson and the great-grandson of preachers. Yes, I see the church as the body of Christ."[16] King's love for the church caused him to evaluate critically the church's role in the struggle for justice and civil rights. In many ways the church failed him and the people of God by being co-opted by the power brokers and the architects of the status quo. All of this made King very weary, but never hopeless.

King's life is an eloquent example of how the preacher's self-understanding is critical to the practice of preaching and doing ministry that will reflect an internalized understanding of the meaning of God and Jesus Christ in his or her life. For King and other Black preachers, it is clear that the Christian religion as embodied in the life of Jesus and the church is ultimately about liberation and reconciliation. Liberation is not implied and usually is not inferred from the term *reconciliation*, but reconciliation without liberation is too easy and too unchristian, too theoretical and idealistic. The mandate of Jesus as metaphor and symbol of liberation is primary and reconciliation is secondary to *communitas*. That interpretation is found in the text from Luke, "The Spirit of the Lord is upon me, because he has chosen me to bring good news to the poor. He has sent me to proclaim *liberty* to the captives and recovery of sight to the blind, to set free the oppressed and announce that the time has come when the Lord will save his people" (Luke 4:18–19, TEV, emphasis mine).

The Self in Community

As King's example illustrates so eloquently, the self-understanding of the preacher shapes and centers his or her relationship to the social and political realities of racism or injustice, just as it does to the church. In the Black church, we are frayed and fragmented, torn and tattered by a slave mentality and by a bourgeois mentality of individualism that strikes at the heart of group unity, of peoplehood, of a new understanding of our faith and commitment to Jesus Christ. But in spite of all the discord and division and the focus on self and individualism at the expense and to the exclusion of the community, God our maker has called us to be unified. The

Black preacher's self-understanding, therefore, is often expressed in terms of the good of unity, and preaching in the Black church advocates unity and especially community. Yet what is community?

Dietrich Bonhoeffer began his discussion of the concept of community in *Life Together* by quoting from the Psalmist: "How very good and pleasant it is when kindred live together in unity!" (Psalm 133:1, NRSV). The concepts of good and unity permeate both *Life Together* and *Ethics*, and this one verse brings these two concepts together. However, in practice, it is often difficult to see the good and to smell the sweetness of unity in the community and the church. One looks around, trying to meander through the culture, through the songs so often sung in the church, through the beliefs and practices of people. One tries to sift through the experiences, through the literature, through the news, through the prayers and testimonies of the faithful—looking everywhere for signs, for statistics, for evidence of unity, looking to see if what one reads and hears and smells is worthy to behold. Instead, there are some other things that one too often sees and smells, and they are neither good nor pleasant.

We read of violent crime and disunity in the community and of bickering and battering by the politicos—that's not good! One of our foremost modern-day Civil Rights leaders, Jesse Jackson, is now saying publicly that he fears Black teenagers. This is a man who put his life on the line for the past thirty years, marching, going to jail, fighting for justice, and fighting the "powers that be" so Black folk could vote, live in decent housing, and secure an equal education. And now he, too, is afraid of the street violence—afraid of the youth.

We know that Black people didn't create violence! The nation, the United States was discovered and sustained by violence. The constitution was constructed in the very presence of violence while Thomas Jefferson and James Madison were speaking about freedom and democracy—but to turn on one's own brothers and sisters within the community with guns, profanity, and violence gets us nowhere but deeper and deeper in a hole. Not only do I read, but also I hear the disunity, the violence, the ugly and evil words. I hear them on television, radio, on records and tapes—I hear the four-letter words, the disrespect, the "dissing" of brothers and sisters by each other. I see it on videos, in hallways, at restaurants and other places.

Everywhere I turn, everywhere I look, everywhere I go, I see the youth mesmerized by the doctors who are not really doctors—doctors who would not know a brain from a kidney, a vein from an artery—doctors who would not know the basic principles of Martin Luther King or Malcolm X, doctors who do not show that they are concerned about life and living it more abundantly. What kind of doctor is Doctor Dre? Doctor Dre, the gangsta rapper, is no more of a doctor than Dr. J, the basketball player, was. He's no more of a doctor than Aretha Franklin's Dr. Feel Good. If these so-called doctors and their associates are the only ones "snooping and dogging" around with one's children, no wonder we have a society that is floundering in a sea of violence, a land of corruption and self-destruction and hate. No wonder there is pain and problems—young people sounding like gangsters, talking *sweet* and acting hip, "dissing" each other about what is "gag" and what is not.

The Black church is in basically the same condition. Folk are fighting each other, one auxiliary trying to outdo another, one choir thinking it's better than another. There is the same rivalry that resulted in one student shot dead and another critically wounded in a dormitory at a prominent and predominantly Black college last year. I'm thankful to God Almighty that in the church, we have not stooped to the lowest level of physical murder—but in the church, there are those who murder each other with their tongue and lips, who kill with their attitude, who maim and maul with their gossip, their lies, their hate, their envy. Martin Luther, the great reformer, said over four hundred years ago, "Where there are dissension, divisions, and discord there is the dwelling of Satan." Disunity is rampant, and the Bible gives us examples of brothers not standing together: Cain and Abel, Jacob and Esau, Joseph and his brothers, Absalom and the other sons of David. While disunity is rampant, Psalm 133 commends and encourages unity as an ideal: unity in worship, unity in family, and unity in society. Togetherness, being in the presence of others, being on one accord, loving one another—is that too much to ask of the church?

To stand together, to be unified, to be united, to be together in unity is a "sweet thing." It is beautiful, delightful. And so the Psalmist says, "How very good and pleasant it is when kindred live together in unity!" One knows how ugly and painful the hate, the dissension, the gossip, the backbiting, the whispers, the disunity. We know how baneful and hateful, how obnoxious and mendacious, how rude and crude, how callous and crazy the people even in the church can act. And yet it is a community—a community in disunion with its creator and each other. This disunion is a prelude to unity, a necessary precondition to solidarity and union with Jesus Christ, which is the ultimate goal of life.

Unity as Gift of the Spirit

> Spare no effort to make fast with bonds of peace the unity which the spirit gives.
> —Ephesians 4:3, NEB

There is a relationship between disruption and stability, and that relationship often fosters unity. Frequently, tension and disruption oscillate with stability in my experience in leadership, particularly as it relates to the church. Whenever there is history of homogeneity, there is a need to create disruption in order that the other can become a reality. This other may be an attenuated form of what is, or it may represent a cataclysmic metamorphosis or transformation of what is.

Disruption, then, is a blessing insofar as it fosters self-examination and change. Disruption is often a constitutive element of change—or a necessary concomitant of the change process. Disruption often creates future stability, and stability is an elemental characteristic of unity. In other words, when two or more things become one, the death of the other becomes imminent.

Unity by its very nature, as a process of creation, represents death as a usurping of the formative other. Unity implies identity and sameness and possibly homogeneous behaviors, actions, and beliefs, often at the expense of the created other. In this sense, unity has a *negative* dimension that we don't often consider in practice. We tend to laud unity as ideal, as a virtue, or as the *telos* of organizational behavior, without considering its inherent flaws.

On the positive side, unity also means togetherness, being of one accord, living in connection with one another as deeply as love and life allow. This is the meaning of unity, yet we are frequently so torn and disjointed in our thinking and in our practices—in our lives—on our jobs, in schools, at home, and at church. Can it be said that we have togetherness in our families, on our streets, in our schools, in the church and community when there is constant discord, disrespect for leadership and life, constant violence, and self-hatred among God's people? This self-hatred manifests itself in acting out our aggression against folk who look just like we look; self-hatred, this lack of unity within self and community, manifests itself in rage that we see among our own people, against one another. Indeed, unity in the body of Christ, the church, is more a hope than a reality. In Ephesians 4:1–16, there is a desire for unity, a theory of unity that in fact has not been achieved, not even to this day. The people of God are to make "every effort to maintain the unity of the Spirit in the bond of peace" (verse 3, NRSV). This unity is a gift of God, an endowment, a talent.

Aesthetic Selving

Communities are repositories of being together, that is, the self in relation and proximity to others. William Desmond says, "The self, even in its singular idiocy, serves as a self for the other. Neither above nor below, neither within nor without, is there escape from community. Community is the very milieu in which self-surpassing and transcendence come to form and fruit."[17] While community is a being together, this does not suggest uniformity but rather the freedom of diversity.

This experience of self in community stands in contrast to Descartes's *cogito ergo sum*, where the self is grounded in thinking to the exclusion of other actions. Since Descartes, white theologians have often been preoccupied with the "disappearing self."[18] But why not "I feel, therefore I am," or "I love, therefore I am," or "I protest, therefore I am," or "I do, therefore I am"?

After all, the essence of being is the bodied self. There is no self apart from the body. *Human being* implies body if nothing else, and the body has an "isness" to it that exists unto itself yet is in community with others. Being in community with others gives the self an otherness that is not obviated by its idiotic inwardness. The self still has an "I am–ness" that is integral to its own bodily incarnation. William Desmond says:

> The incarnate body is a fleshed "I am" which is also an "I am with." For the "I am" could not otherwise be also a "Here I am" were not the other already implicated in the elemental affirmation of the self. The incarnate "I am" is an immediate certainty of self-presence, a self-certainty before all concepts of itself. To put it this way is already too abstract, since

this self-certainty is just the immediate, lived intimacy of the self in relation to itself. Immediate self-relation in the aesthetic body: this hyphen of self-relation is important: it signals a space of otherness from the beginning: self-relation is also self-differing.[19]

There is no self apart from this aesthetic self of mind and body, consciousness and unconsciousness, sensuality and reflection. The bodily self is the seat of human life with all of its antecedent expressions and feelings of joy and suffering.

It seems that the aesthetic self is constituted and mediated by desire, imagination, and memory. While desire seems to be more a component of the erotic self, imagination is the component of self that promises liberation and freedom. Desmond, in referring to desire and imagination, respectively, says,

> The first registers the exterior and the body's interchange with it. The second articulates the power within the self to generate from its own resources the shape of its response to being, whether inner or outer. Desire sends us in search of ourselves and the other, imagination allows us to begin to articulate explicitly the shape of that sought self and the other.[20]

This notion of desire suggests that the self is often reflected and fulfilled in the other, especially the other that precisely correlates with the self. However, it is the explication of the component of self as *imagination* that intrigues me as an African American whose ancestors were slaves in the antebellum South. Desmond's assertion that imagination "articulates the power within the self to generate from its own resources the shape of its response to being, whether inner or outer" speaks volumes to an oppressed, shackled, and deontologized people.

Desmond is right when he says that *desire* and *imagination* are allies. They are highly correlated in any quest for freedom of the body and mind. Imagination allows the self to envision a world where there is justice and freedom, a world where there are no more chains and all God's children are free. This was the reason why slaves could survive their status as chattel—a commodity on par with farm animals such as cattle and horses. (By the way, the animals were allowed to rest, while the slaves labored from sunup to sundown.) This is unlike Hannah Arendt's notion of work, because the slaves could not barter and exchange and had no control over the produce of their hands.[21] Imagination provides the self with the communicative tool to "reconfigure reality."[22]

It is precisely this reconfigured reality served by imagination that Desmond also describes. He states:

> For imagination is original. It originates in the self the opening to the other as other by opening up the self as the free power of self-articulation. It does this in the aesthetic body, but in the process transcends it. Consider: if we could not imagine in the free sense intended, we could never imagine what it would be like to be different to what one presently is . . . Imagination is a power that releases our original identification of difference. While remaining myself, I imagine the inner being of the other as other. I may even *become that being as other* by assuming through imitation what I imagine that other to be. Similarly, through that same free power I can imagine *myself as other*. I dream of as yet unrealized possibility that I vaguely sense is slumbering in the present self. Thus imagination is central to the genesis, the determinate articulation, and the creative formation of any career of self transcendence.[23]

Inherent in and integral to imagination is possibility, and possibility is grounded in dreaming and self-transcendence. The ability to not be burdened and limited by the existing self also speaks of an equivocalness that is an inherent component of the aesthetic self.

Additionally, imagination may in fact be the first step toward faith and belief in God. The ability and power to imagine is a transcendent reality in the sense of hope for a transformed human existence. Moreover, the ability to imagine another world and to dream a new existence is the hallmark of Black life as expressed particularly through the preacher. Martin Luther King's "I Have a Dream" speech is a classic reconfiguring and reinterpretation of the condition of existence for whites and African Americans. King's dream imagines a new reality for everybody. Imagination enables the unimagining self also to imagine and help to create a new reality. Imagination is a necessary hermeneutic tool in the development of any theology or ethic, whether systematic or constructive.

The following sermon illustrates preaching informed by self-understanding. As you read, consider how my message is informed by my experiences as I have described them in this chapter. What experiences have shaped your own understanding of who you are, as well as your congregation's self-understanding? Where do you find the congregation's unity and its moral imperative? Where is its dream? Are these expressed authentically in your own preaching?

Sermon *Everybody's Talking*

> He went down to Capernaum, a city in Galilee, and was teaching them on the sabbath. They were astounded at his teaching, because he spoke with authority. In the synagogue there was a man who had the spirit of an unclean demon, and he cried out with a loud voice, "Let us alone! What have

you to do with us, Jesus of Nazareth? Have you come to
destroy us? I know who you are, the Holy One of God." But
Jesus rebuked him, saying, "Be silent, and come out of him!"
When the demon had thrown him down before them, he
came out of him without having done him any harm. They
were all amazed and kept saying to one another, "What kind
of utterance is this? For with authority and power he commands the unclean spirits, and out they come!" And a report
about him began to reach every place in the region.
    —Luke 4:31–37, NRSV

In the summer of 1955, Emmett Till, a recently turned fourteen-year-old Black boy from Chicago, boarded a bus with
the help of his mother to visit family and friends in Money,
Mississippi. This would be the last time that he would see
Chicago alive, because on a hot August day, Emmett Till and
seven of his friends went into a corner store in the Mississippi
Delta to get a drink, a soda pop to refresh their thirst, and
being a rather rambunctious and curious adolescent boy,
Emmett Till whistled at Carolyn Bryant, the white wife of the
store's owner. A little commotion broke out, but they were
able to get out of the store and go home. But word spread of
the whistling incident, and a few days later in the early
morning hours, a group of white men carrying guns and
flashlights came to the house where Emmett Till was staying
and dragged him off and bludgeoned him to death—beating
his body to a pulp and then shooting him in the head and
dumping his mutilated and mangled body into the Talla-
hatchie River with a seventy-five-pound cotton gin fan tied
around his neck.

    The two white men who went on trial for Emmett's death,
Ray Bryant and J. W. Milam, were both acquitted after a five-
day trial with an all-white jury that deliberated for just over an
hour. I was only three years old during that summer of 1955,

and I don't know how or when I learned of the violent effects of racism and injustice in this nation, but I know that as long as I can remember, this evil and demonic act of hatred, racism, and injustice has been etched in my mind and on my heart.

Emmett Till's fourteen-year-old body was carried back to Chicago, and his mother, Mamie Till, decided to let the whole world see how cruel and evil white racism could be by allowing her son's body to lie in an open casket during the funeral. Fifty thousand people marched past, seeing firsthand the demonic and evil ravages of a racist society and how that evil spirit manifested itself against African Americans. To kill a fourteen-year-old Black boy for "horsing around" with his friends and in the process daring to whistle or to speak playfully to a white woman was indicative of the sick and evil nature of racism in America. This sickness and evil permeated every segment of our society from the criminal justice system, the courts, the law, the schools, businesses, housing, transportation, etc. to the sanctuaries of the white church in America.

Everybody was talking about the death of Emmett Till, but there had been two other recent lynchings in Mississippi. These terrorist acts had seen the Rev. George Lee lynched at Belzoni, Mississippi, after he and Gus Court attempted to register to vote in Humphreys County. And Lamar Smith was lynched in Brookhaven, Mississippi.[24]

And just a few months later, on December 1, 1955, in Montgomery, Alabama, not too far from Money, Mississippi, Rosa Parks refused to give up her seat to a white man on the public bus. The Montgomery bus boycott sparked a sense of resistance and hope that launched Dr. Martin Luther King Jr. into the public square as the leader of the modern Civil Rights Movement.

Dr. Martin Luther King Jr., born January 15, 1929, died on April 4, 1968, at the hands of an assassin's bullet in Memphis, Tennessee. Dr. King would never forget the evil act of violence perpetrated against Emmett Till in Money, Mississippi, because out of all the places he feared going, he most feared Mississippi because of her blatant and evil acts of racism and injustice. And the word on the street was that King was to be shot on sight if he even stepped on Mississippi soil.

The word spread fast that day when this slender, quiet, dignified woman, Rosa Parks, was arrested for defying the racist segregation laws of Montgomery, Alabama. Everybody throughout the south and nation was talking about it—people felt proud of her strength, her defiant spirit was so biblical, so Christlike, so much an act of personhood, an ontological statement, the embodiment of an ethical stance about justice and human dignity. Rosa Parks was saying, "I am somebody," "I count for something," "I work for a living, I pay taxes, I have a right, I am tired of being treated like dirt, like an animal!" This powerful act of freedom started everybody talking—folk were whispering, chattering, talking about this woman, and when Dr. Martin Luther King Jr. spoke at the first public service trying to rally support for the bus boycott, there was more talk.

Everybody was talking about this twenty-six-year-old Baptist preacher who spoke with such knowledge and assurance, such passion and compassion, such an understanding of the plight of African American people. King talked of love and nonviolent protest; he said, "Injustice anywhere is a threat to justice everywhere," and, "Justice delayed is justice denied," and,

> In the midst of blatant injustices inflicted upon the Negro, I have watched white churches stand on the sideline and merely mouth pious irrelevancies and sanctimonious trivialities. In the midst of a mighty struggle to rid our nation of racial and economic injustice, I have heard so many ministers say, "Those are social issues with which the gospel has

no real concern," and I have watched so many churches commit themselves to a completely otherworldly religion which made a strange distinction between body and soul, the sacred and the secular. So here we are . . . with a religious community largely adjusted to the status quo, standing as a tail light behind other community agencies rather than a headlight leading men to higher levels of justice.[25]

Folk were talking in the Black community. Folk were feeling hopeful and scared. They were talking about this preacher—maybe he was crazy, he was so smart, so smooth, so eloquent, so brave in his speech and in his acts. He stared the devil, the evil system of segregation and injustice in the face, and called the demon to come out of America. He encouraged Black people to resist being treated with indignity and injustice and to fight for freedom. Just as Black men are the ones to fight first and lose their lives first in a war, they are the ones who fill our prisons and jails, yet so many people oppose affirmative action.

In our text today, everybody's talking because Jesus has just put into practice what he had said earlier. Jesus was in Capernaum, a town in Galilee, teaching the people on the Sabbath. They were amazed by his teaching because he taught with authority. There was a man in the synagogue who had a spirit of an evil demon in him. The man or the demon in the man screamed out in a loud voice saying, "What do you want with us, Jesus of Nazareth? Are you here to destroy us? I know who you are. You are God's Holy messenger!" Jesus orders the spirit to be quiet and come out of the man, and the evil spirit is obedient to the voice of Jesus, throws the man to the floor, and comes out of him without hurting the man. Everybody sees this, and they are amazed and begin to say to one another, "What kind of words are these?" or, "What a word!" With authority and power, Jesus gives orders to the evil spirits, and they obey, "and people everywhere began to spread the news of Jesus' work" (Luke 4:31–37).

Jesus is first of all a teacher of the word of God, and that word has power. It is the power of the word that causes such a stir. People are amazed by his teaching—they are astounded, amazed, flabbergasted—amazed at the way he taught because he taught with authority. He spoke with authority—not with tepid trepidation, but with authority—not with fear and trembling, tiptoeing around certain issues of justice and righteousness, issues of love and peace, but he spoke with authority—not with halting doubt and skepticism, but with assurance and faith. He spoke with authority—both epistemic and moral authority. Jesus knew who he was, and he knew that his authority came from God, and because he was fully God and fully man, he could teach and speak the word. Jesus is an expert in the word. His teaching is the essence of the moral, the good, the just, the fair, the right. That's why Jesus could speak to the demonic spirit in the man, and the spirit obeyed him. The demon recognized Jesus as the Holy One of God.

Jesus speaks and demonstrates authority over the demon and heals the man. While Jesus continued to have trouble with the hard-heartedness of humans who threaten to kill him, the demon recognizes and obeys him as the holy one of God. His authority resides in who he is—God's holy messenger. So he orders the spirit to "Be quiet and come out of the man!" The spirit obeys, and the man is healed.

Some of us need the same healing today! I don't know what evil spirit runs rampant in your heart and mind. I don't know what demons you are fighting in your life, in your body, in your mind—whether it's mental illness, paranoia, drug abuse, identity issues, mental abuse, sexual abuse, spousal abuse, child abuse, alcohol abuse—whatever your addictions, your pains, your struggles. It could be gambling or stealing. It could be lying, cheating, backstabbing, deceit, double-talk, double cross—whatever demon haunts and harasses you today, whatever throws you down and wrestles you to the ground can come out of you, and by the word of God, you too can be healed—you can walk away from here today healed—made whole, freed from your demons—free from your addiction, free from your habits, free from whatever has a strong hold on your life, whatever oppresses and obstructs your well-being.

The text says when the people saw what Jesus said and did, they were again amazed and said to one another, "What kind of words are these?" or, "What a word is this!" What a word is this! What a word! A word of deliverance and transformation. What a word! A word spoken in love—what a word! A word of power, a word that pricks the consciousness. What a word! A word that causes the demons to obey. What a word. A word that knocks you down and picks you up again! What a word. A word that won't do you any harm, but a word that heals! What a word. A word that cuts like a two-edged sword. A word that calms your fears and soothes your soul—what a word. A word that controls your tongue and your temper—what a word. A word that comforts my spirit and calms my tongue. What a word, a word of authority and power, the spoken word. Because Jesus speaks, we too can speak. We can speak to the conditions of our own lives and our culture—to the demons and the evil spirits—and cast them out! What a word is this.

Jesus' word is our word. His word is a lamp unto my feet, a light unto my pathway. What a word. This word will make you love your enemies and pray for those who persecute you—what a word! It will make you forgive your neighbor. What a word! It will make you say, "I am sorry." What a word! It will make you cry sometimes, and sometimes it will make you shout for joy. What a word. This word will make you get on your knees and pray. It will make you shout. It will make you holler! What a word!

2

The Preaching of the Elders:
Princes of the African American Pulpit

I heard de preachin' of de Elder,
Preachin' de Word, preachin' de Word.
I heard de preachin' of de Elder, preachin' de word o' God. Yes,
preachin' de word o' God.
—Negro spiritual

In light of the importance we have ascribed to the preacher's self-understanding, I offer in this chapter an overview of three modern African American princes of the pulpit. Each has something vital to offer about the kind of preaching I commend in this volume, and each has had a direct impact on my own life and ministry. Dr. John M. Ellison was my catechist during my preparation for ordination, Dr. Miles Jerome Jones my preaching teacher in seminary, and Dr. Samuel Proctor my mentor and adviser for the doctorate in preaching and African American church studies. These three giants of the African American pulpit and the classroom have helped to shape the preaching tradition throughout the nation. They especially have had a lasting and positive influence on my life and preaching, and I hope others will benefit from the following thoughts about them as preachers and teachers of preachers.

John Malcus Ellison:
The Personality and Interpretive Mind
of the Preacher

John Malcus Ellison, born in Northumberland County, Virginia, in 1889, is one of the early heroes of African American education as well as the African American church. Ellison received his bachelor's degree from Virginia Union University, his seminary training at Oberlin Theological Seminary, and his doctorate in sociology of religion from Drew University. Ellison would eventually—and to some extent by default—in 1941 become the first African American president of historic Virginia Union University. Known for his significant contributions as an academician, preacher, university president, and civil rights activist, Ellison was also known for being a teacher of preachers. It has often been said that during his lifetime an individual's calling was not legitimate until Ellison placed his stamp of approval on that person. Revered by many, Ellison was a true classicist by all accounts; however, Miles Jones in reflecting on Ellison said that he was quite emotional and much less stoic than he is generally perceived to have been. He wanted the preacher to be an amalgamation of form and substance.

One of the primary concerns for Dr. Ellison, drawing on his background in sociology, was the preacher as person. For Ellison, the preacher was more than just that individual who stood up in the pulpit each Sunday, delivering a message. The preacher, though human and full of faults, was to be the example of how a Christian should live in this sinful world. Ellison states, "Many people look to him [the preacher] as their ideal."[1] In his book *They Who Preach*, Ellison expresses his belief that the preacher's calling is the most noble of all vocations.[2] As a result of that calling, he felt the preacher must be a person of deep humility. Ellison suggests that the ministry is not a job that is geared toward receiving personal gain and glory on earth:

> The ministry is the highest of all callings but because it is sometimes invaded by men whose motives are not entirely free from the desire for selfish advantage such men are not easily or quickly detected. It is understandable, though that the ministry is thus sometimes invaded. The minister has the position of unusual prominence and influence. Rarely do men of other professions rise so quickly to esteem and attention as the minister of rare gifts. He is more widely known and more acclaimed than other men in the community. There are men of less influence who desire the recognition and power, which they feel a minister has. Thus the Christian ministry is vulnerable to many false prophets who see the ministry as a quick avenue to popularity and power.[3]

Ellison gives a stern reminder that the individual should not be in the ministry for personal glory but rather to give God glory. He has a very high estimation of human responsibility that should correspond with the high calling to preach the gospel.

Ellison believed that the preacher must have integrity. One aspect of integrity is being honest, and he believed that a person called into the ministry should possess honesty.[4] Ellison states, "No man is obligated to be great, wise or popular, but every man is obligated to be honest."[5] Honesty is an ethical trait that should be practiced. It is an obligation, a moral duty and a stand to which the minister must adhere.

J. M. Ellison further believed that the preacher must possess a spirit of unselfishness. Accordingly, the preacher is a "man bigger than self." Dr. Ellison believed that an effective preacher is one who can direct the attention of the people away from him- or herself.[6] This ability to not be self-absorbed and to be directed toward the other is a mark of effectiveness on the part of the preacher.

Another essential element of the personhood of the preacher according to Ellison is scholarship. The preacher must be not only a scholar of religion, but also a scholar of other aspects of life. Therefore, Ellison believed that it would take a lifetime to achieve such scholarship.[7] This emphasis on lifelong learning is the mark of a serious preacher of the gospel. Dr. Ellison believed that the preacher ought to be able to stand with other individuals of various fields and be able to converse and dialogue with them, thus receiving the respect of others as a result of his of her scholarship.[8] He states, "The minister's breadth of view should include many areas of knowledge. He must learn to live at the crossroads where these areas meet and be able to relate them to the problems of living. History, philosophy, science, sociology, economics, literature, and art ought to be areas of knowledge in which he is at home. To all these areas of knowledge, he must bring the critical, interpretive mind. Knowing is an important tool for the minister's work."[9]

Samuel DeWitt Proctor: The Ethical Dimensions of a Sermon

Samuel DeWitt Proctor, who earned a doctorate in Christian ethics from Boston University, was heavily influenced by the ethical questions found in the Bible and the issues that individuals struggle with on a daily basis. Thus, the major themes found throughout his sermons often pose an ethical problem. Being a champion of justice and equality, Proctor emphasized the necessity for individuals to make decisions that are just and fair when dealing with one another. He would often say in classes and seminars that the preacher should deal with serious life-and-death issues, not small textual issues such as whether it is feasible to expect a camel to go through the eye of a needle.

Proctor also felt that the preacher could not afford to focus on the small and sometimes nebulous concerns people have. The preacher is compelled to address the complex and difficult issues of life. Proctor considered people's minor concerns to be unimportant—ancillary, sidebar issues that too often occupied the minds of preachers and churchgoers. He would say that the preacher needs to be well grounded and not gullible in the sense of being lured into preaching about that which is unimportant and nontransforming.

Moreover, Proctor would often say, "The sermon must be portable." He believed that the gospel speaks to persons of all backgrounds and understanding; therefore, it has portability. The sermon must be the same way. It can be preached in California and in Virginia and be equally effective in both places as long as the preacher takes into consideration the local congregational context.

In his book *The Certain Sound of the Trumpet: Crafting a Sermon of Authority,* Proctor uses his own sermons to illustrate his principles for a sound theological sermon with ethical implications. One of the sermons he uses is based on the parable of the Good Samaritan. The central idea that Proctor attempts to share with listeners and readers is the necessity for individuals to be compassionate toward one another despite differences in their racial or economic class. The issue of compassion and treating individuals the way in which one would desire to be treated is a ubiquitous ethical issue that persons are faced with daily.[10] Each person faces two choices: Does one treat persons unjustly because of their social status? Or does one look past other people's social status in order to see them as God would see them?

The issue of equality was dear to Proctor, who was a product of segregation. He understood what it was like to be the man left for dead on the Jericho road. In his autobiography, *The Substance of Things Hoped For: A Memoir of African-*

American Faith, Proctor shares a story of his days working as a navy shipfitter's apprentice. While Proctor was taking a drink of water from the faucet, one of his older white colleagues commented that he should not be drinking from the faucet on the right but from the faucet on the left. The white colleague further commented, "All coloreds use the left fountain."[11] Incidents such as this reminded Proctor of where African Americans stood with America during that time period[12] and that segregation was both immoral and unequal.

Another example of Proctor's use of ethical issues to challenge his readers and listeners can be found in his sermon about the parable of the talents. The title of this sermon is "The Blessings That We Forget." His central argument is that individuals ought to be treated fairly and justly because God has treated us in the same manner. Proctor suggests that people tend to receive grace and forgiveness from others, yet when the opportunity arises for them to do likewise, persons are not as quick to forgive. Once again, ethical issues confront the listeners and readers because persons are challenged either to continue expressing selfishness or to be the example of Christ and forgive others just as God has forgiven us.[13]

Miles Jerome Jones:
On Being an Authentic Preacher

Miles Jones was a teacher and mentor to the very end of his life. He was a man of strength, integrity, and character, and these attributes emanated from his being, his ontological essence in the way that he coped with his impending death. He taught classes, kept office hours, read students' papers, and met with the homiletics faculty about his teaching methodology in light of his realistic view of his health—thus his death. Because he knew that he was dying and his illness (cancer) was becoming more aggressive and unrelenting on his body, he openly discussed his situation, saying to us, "I don't think I am going to make it, brothers." Without skipping a beat, he then went on to the next topic, which was to discuss his teaching method with us in order that we could meet the existing demands of the homiletics teaching schedule. This meant that there would be a shared and collaborative effort to teach the introductory homiletics course to approximately one hundred students. For three or four weeks, we met and talked about the course—discussing its content, how to encourage students without misleading them, the importance of the preaching courses in the curriculum, and some other personal and academic issues unique to Virginia Union University. This entire process, in retrospect, was a type of real-life lesson before dying.

In the first line of Ernest Gaines's classic novel *A Lesson before Dying*, the words "*I was not there*, yet I was there" seem to capture the way I felt during the last days of Miles Jerome Jones's life. There is something transcendent about the statement, moving us beyond time and space. This is Black consciousness and identification with the soul and suffering of another. It is the same way I felt about the death of my father and my mother, who passed away in 1988 and 1989, respectively. My father succumbed to heart disease and on a hot day in August slumped over in my sister's house and died. Our mother fell to the ravages of colon cancer; with dignity, quiet, and without complaint, she slipped away in the middle of the night less than a year after my father died. These experiences are forever etched into my memory, creating a void and a sadness from which I cannot fully escape. I thought I had dealt with the pain and the loss of my biological parents until Miles Jerome Jones died, and I felt a similar loss and pain. He was so much like a father—a wise counselor to me and many, many others in ministry.

However, this section is about his preaching style and interpretative homiletic method. I have often referred to him as a philosophical preacher par excellence, one who grounded his homiletics in both hermeneutics and philosophy. He was very much interested in what he termed "the practice of preaching." What he meant by this is a type of metaphysics of practice—the foundational elements involved in the practice of preaching, that is, putting the sermon together and presenting it to the congregation on a regular basis.

Being a Preacher

At the time of his death in December 2002, Miles Jerome Jones was a prince of a preacher and the senior homiletics teacher at the School of Theology, Virginia Union University in Richmond. He was perhaps the seminary's best-kept secret, and his popularity pales in comparison to his impact upon his homiletics students. Though not well published, he was a scholar and practitioner of the word who was influenced by John M. Ellison, Sandy F. Ray, Samuel Proctor, Paul Tillich, David Buttrick, James Cone, Howard Thurman, and Thomas Long.[14] His teaching and preaching contributed much to theological reflection and understanding, particularly in the area of homiletics. He was, in my view, a prince of the African American pulpit, whose eloquent words and polished demeanor drew the listener into his grasp as the sweet aroma of the gospel was being preached. He was an artist of the word, an architect of the sentence and the sermon. But his real focus was on the preacher's understanding of existence and being.

Where much of homiletic inquiry focuses on sermon craftsmanship, Jones turned his attention to the *being* of the preacher and offered a critical assessment of what it means to *be* a preacher. This hermeneutic of being or essence was exhibited as much in his persona as in the words he used to convey his understandings. Those who sat under the tutelage of Jones memorized the definition of a sermon, and with an almost rhythmic response could uniformly repeat a definition that he borrowed from James Wall and that James Wall got from G. Ray Jordan in his book, *The Art of Preaching*: "A sermon is a statement of faith, drawn from the context of tradition, projecting the authentic being of the preacher."[15] This was the crux of Jones's teaching and one of the first things a new seminarian was taught. What does this mean? How does this definition encapsulate Jones' hermeneutic of *being* as it relates to the preacher?

Jones's homiletical hermeneutics, ontological theories, and understanding of self were largely influenced by theologian Paul Tillich. For Miles Jones there was a correlation between preaching and being that is just like the correlation between scripture and situation of existence. Tillich's correlational typology also facilitated Jones's interest in the African American's condition of existence and society's effort to relegate African Americans to a state of *nonbeing*. This is where he found Tillich to be helpful. Being, for Tillich, is the actualized power of God to overcome nonbeing.[16] All of being is grounded in God, and God is that which constitutes ultimacy, that is, ultimate concern.[17] Where there is being, there is, as Jones would say, the presence of the Divine.

Jones believed that the being of the preacher is as significant to the sermon as the words themselves. In this sense, he would agree with Phillips Brooks that preaching is "truth through personality." Jones would say, "Don't think that what's on the paper is the full sermon!" Furthermore, he interpreted the sermon as a reflection of who the preacher is. This would suggest that for Jones there is no dichotomy between the being of the preacher and the act of preaching. This puts him in the company of Dietrich Bonhoeffer. While there may not be a dichotomy, there is a dialectic between act and being, and Jones sought to synthesize act and being through the preached word.[18] The sermon as a statement only, according to

Jones's teaching, begs for an expression of performance that validates the exhortation and affirms the imperative that is implied in the proclamation itself. The preacher is called to be an active participant in that expression to show forth the essence of the self in presenting the preached word.

Further evidence of Tillich's influence is seen in Jones's working definition of preaching: "Preaching is the action that creates the avenue for love's entrance into human affairs." Tillich's work on being is developed as it is actualized through love, power, and justice. Tillich defines life as being in actuality and love as the moving power of life.[19] Moreover, being is not actual without the love which drives everything that is.[20] There is an analogous correlation between the aim of love's work in being and the aim of love's work in preaching. In both, the work of love seeks to unite that which is separated and functions as the power that urges a reuniting response from the listener in the encountered reality of being and nonbeing. Applying Tillich's terms, Jones describes this power as actualized being that is made manifest, that is, realized when it comes against another entity.[21] In other words, being is not being until being confronts the other, either in self or another. In his lectures, Jones defined power as the pure expression of being.[22] Thus, the being of the preacher is actualized power whose existence is predicated upon the encounter with the other through the act of preaching.

Jones's three-part definition of a sermon represents the multidimensional nature of the message. To understand Miles Jones and, more importantly, his interpretation of being a preacher, it is necessary to examine this definition. The three parts—statement of faith, context of tradition, and projection of the preacher's authentic being—fully construct Jones's hermeneutic of being and more particularly of being a preacher.

As a statement of faith, the sermon is the communicated beliefs of the preacher.[23] The preacher simply (or rather not so simply) uses words as shells for meaning to communicate interpretations of things as they relate to the Divine.[24] A particular characteristic of Miles Jones was certainly his appreciation for words and the artistry with which he used words to convey meaning—what he saw, what he meant, how he felt, and who he was. This understanding of a sermon as art was based on the theories of I. A. Richards, who was considered by some to be the father of literary criticism.[25] Jones as a preacher was himself an artist, and the manuscript was his canvas upon which to stroke words that together painted his interpretation of the Divine. Jones was as emphatic about the words used as the faith being communicated by their use: "Words are a preacher's stock and barrel . . . What we are obliged to do when we preach is to unpack words. Preachers do not have the luxury of holding on to a concept that they cannot articulate."[26] Therefore, the faith communicated is only as effective as the words used to describe it. Without the words, packaged in a way that yields the transference of a shared faith, faith is not faith. Because the aim of power and love is reunion, the self is always looking for itself. Therefore, the listener, like the preacher, is looking for self in the sermon. The art of the sermon must be expressed by the artist in hopes of identifying the common thread that listeners can relate to.[27] This is the reunion, the uniting of self with self, being with being, and self with other or, as Paul Ricoeur would say, oneself as another.[28]

Miles Jones understood faith to be something that the preacher believes, not just a cognitive awareness or intellectual assent. It is something that the preacher is willing to trust in order to move forward.[29] Faith, as Jones defined it, is that upon which I cast my full weight.[30] Faith, then, was understood by

Jones as being grounded in a personal interpretation of the reality of the Divine, a conviction for which there is no proof.[31] The statement of faith is drawn from the context of tradition. This means that any statement of one's faith is drawn out of the text (that is, scripture) and the context.[32] The preacher uses the biblical text as a springboard into the sermon. The events and stories of the Bible are used to uncover issues and truths for modern society. The method of interpretation is called "figural," for the Bible and contemporary experience take the shape of a single, enormous tapestry whose figures are repeated in many locations with a variety of significations.[33] The interpreter (preacher plus community) decodes the pattern as it occurs in contemporary events by means of a divinely given spiritual discernment.[34] The Bible mirrors or contains all of life, and life mirrors or replicates the figures and stories of the Bible.[35] The use of the text is coupled with the particular context of the preacher—the events and circumstances that inform the preacher's understanding and unequivocally affect the preacher's interpretation of everything that is being communicated in the sermon.

The final element of the definition of a sermon is the projection of the authentic being of the preacher. The statement of faith, drawn from the context of the tradition, has as its aim the projection of the authentic being of the preacher. For Jones, this further supports his understanding of the intricate relationship between being and the practice of preaching. Authenticity is perhaps the key word, lending itself to a divine act. According to Jones, authenticity depends upon the author, the Divine.[36] Authenticity comes from authority. Thus, the authentic being of the preacher is the being that gives itself over to God.[37] Jones understood the authority of God the Divine as that which enables us to be what we could never be without the power and presence of God.

Kerygmatic Preaching

Miles Jones introduced us to the word *kerygma*. Before him, I had only heard of charisma, so I was intrigued by this new, powerful word, kerygma. Jones felt that preaching should be kerygmatic—that is, embodying the life, death, and resurrection of Jesus Christ. He said, "The church understood this to be essential in every sermon." Kerygma, said Miles Jones, is the identifying characteristic of Christian preaching. This is evident in the Gospels, the book of Acts, and in the Pauline writings. Moreover, preaching demands a response. Jones said, "In preaching, there is a need to respond. No one is preaching just to be preaching, and no one is listening just to be listening."[38] The imperative is to respond!

Let's look briefly at the three elements of kerygmatic preaching, which focus on the life, death, and resurrection of Jesus. Each strand requires interpretation. What is life? Again, Jones appropriated the meaning of life in Tillichian terminology:

> This is what Tillich calls *being* in actuality—a certain way of being in the world. We have to say what His being means. What does it mean to say that "He lives"? What is the hallmark of His being? A daily existence that came into contact with adversity; yet he was never overcome by it (see Mark 14). Jesus is in trouble for no reason except his being.[39]

Again, in discussing kerygma, Jones offered a philosophical interpretation that is grounded in an ontological construction. The fact that Jesus was able to confront adversity without being overcome by it and the reality of his trouble—that is, his persistent antagonists taunting him—is directly correlated with who he was. Moreover, Miles Jones emphasized the importance of interpreting everything:

> Jesus' death has to be interpreted because He didn't just die.
> He was put to death. He was negated. He was put out of
> existence. Death is when one is denied any further extension
> in time and space. Death is the curtailment of life, the nega-
> tion of life.[40]

In describing this second component of kerygma to our class,
Jones seemed to switch gears; his language seemed to shift to
his own impending death. During this conversation, he was
very sick, and I felt that he was reckoning with his own termi-
nal illness as well as explicating the meaning of Jesus' death.
He described death as "denial of further existence."

But, for me, Miles Jones reserves his most succinct eloquence for his definition of resurrection, which is the third and
final element of understanding kerygma. He says resurrection
is "confrontation with negation." It is being in all of its boldness without any semblance of arrogance. In connection with
the third element of kerygma, Jones describes "a being that has
no business being but nevertheless is here. There is no arrogance in resurrection. It is confrontation with negation. The
necessity for resurrected being to be dealt with grows out of
divine humility."[41] This "confrontation with negation" is Miles
Jones's way of explaining resurrection in assertive ontological
terms. Resurrection is not only confrontation with negation as
Jones asserts, but it ultimately defeats and overcomes negation. Herein lies the proleptic vision of hope and the faith and
power to overcome the last enemy, which is death. Resurrection overcomes death. Paul writes, "Death is destroyed; victory
is complete! . . . But thanks be to God who gives us the victory
through our Lord, Jesus Christ!" (1 Corinthians 15:54b, 57, TEV).

The following sermon owes much to what I have learned
from Drs. Ellison, Jones, and Proctor. As you read it, look for
the elements of kerygmatic preaching and an application to

the significant concerns of people's lives. When you preach, what aspects of your own faith and character do you want to communicate along with your words?

◇◇◇

Sermon *From Talk to Testimony*

> Jesus went on with his disciples to the villages of Caesarea Philippi; and on the way he asked his disciples, "Who do people say that I am?" And they answered him, "John the Baptist; and others, Elijah; and still others, one of the prophets." He asked them, "But who do you say that I am?" Peter answered him, "You are the Messiah." And he sternly ordered them not to tell anyone about him.
> —Mark 8:27–30, NRSV

We are a talking people. A chattering group of individuals who often can't wait to tell others what happened in a meeting, what somebody else said about us, or even what we thought we heard. For example, someone may have said to you when you asked what was said, "Child, I couldn't really hear everything, but it seems like I heard them call you this or that. It sounded like they were saying that you sure have put on a lot of weight or ever since she got married, she doesn't even favor herself." You have heard the talk reverberating in the corridors of your school. You have heard talk in places like the barber shop or the beauty salon while your hair is soaked in suds, the curling iron is so close to your scalp that you are afraid to move an inch because you might get nicked or burned, or while you are under the hair dryer straining to hear the latest news about violence in schools, the car tax, the vacillating politicians, the pastor and his wife, the church meeting.

You name it, and somebody is talking about it. We can talk our heads off. Some folk can talk themselves into trouble, and others can talk themselves out of trouble. We live in a talking world, from talk radio to TV talk shows, from Rickie Lake, Sally Jesse Raphael, Jenny Jones, Phil Donahue, Regis and Kelly to Oprah Winfrey and Dr. Phil. We love to hear other folk talk, and we love to talk about ourselves. We don't have to know necessarily what we're talking about to engage in talk. We talk just to be talking—to be in the crowd, to be cool, to be in a special group, to feel accepted, to help others to like us, and to impress others. We want to be a part of the 411 Club. We can rap on the Internet or talk on our cell phones.

We talk about our leaders, our churches, our ministers, our colleagues, our associates, our friends, our coworkers, our bosses. We talk about our love lives, our conquests, and our forays into the illegal and the immoral. We talk about the old, the young, the weak, the strong, the sick, the well, the poor, the rich, the living, and the dead. We love to talk! talk! talk! without any serious regard for truth, justice, fairness, or the feelings and conditions of others. We say, "I heard that he doesn't like old people; they don't have anything for the young people to do; their music is whack; the Holy Spirit hasn't been in that church since . . ."

People in the church do too much unnecessary talking, vain babblings, rumorings, spreading gossip, lies! We love to talk and tell what others said, but too often we refuse to correct a lie or an injustice or to put an end to a rumor and speak the truth straight up, without fear, without stammering, and without wavering, because somehow we love to fuel the wildfire of talk, wagging tongues, just talking incessantly all the time.

Talk is cheap! Jive talk, small talk, just talking to hear ourselves talk. Haven't you seen and heard folk talk about what they would do if . . . or how much better they are at this game or that sport. Some of us often rush home after church to watch the basketball game or the football game or the baseball game, and the whole time the game is being played, we are second-guessing the coach, dissing the players, saying, "Man, I could have made that shot," "I can run faster than that," "How could he miss the ball?" "He must have a hole in that glove," and on and on. Yet when the ball is in fact in our court, and we have to put up or shut up, then we recognize that talk is cheap, talk is easy, talk is something that we must move beyond as a church, as a people, as Christians, and as followers of Jesus Christ.

In Mark 8:27, Jesus and his disciples are at the crossroads. Here at the midpoint of Mark's gospel, Jesus' public ministry in Galilee is basically finished. He has explained the meaning of the Sabbath. He has healed the sick. He's been accused by scribes and Pharisees, yet he has stilled the storm, fed the five thousand with a few fish and a little bread, and given sight to the blind. And now, as all of these miracles are behind him and he begins to move toward Jerusalem, he stands on the precipice of the future. As Jesus and his disciples move toward the villages of Caesarea Philippi from the foothills of Mount Hermon, they get a clear view of Galilee—that is, where they have been—and a not-so-clear view of Jerusalem—that is, where they are going. Galilee represents ministry of healing, but Jerusalem represents suffering and death and resurrection. This very point geographically, theologically, and spiritually is the point where Jesus' disciples must now move from talk to testimony. This move is a spiritual journey, a leap of faith from the general to the specific, from what others say to what they themselves believe. This is akin to where we are today, at the fulcrum of our faith. We are at a point where our future, our faith, and our commitment turn on our answer to two questions: (1) "Who do people say that I am?" and (2) "Who do you say that I am?"

Let us look at these relevant textual questions today, because while both are important, one is general, and the other is specific. Talk is broad; testimony is narrow and particular.

Talk can be attributed to others. It demands no reverent respect, no reason to be right, no long-lasting location in the language of life and faith.

Let's look at the question in verse 27: "Jesus went on with his disciples to the villages of Caesarea Philippi; and on the way," or as he was walking, "he asked his disciples, 'Who do people say that I am?'" In other words, who am I according to the talk of the town? What's the talk, what's the chatter, what's the word on the street? What are people saying about me? Jesus wanted to know what his disciples had heard, and the text says they answered him, "John the Baptist; and others, Elijah; and still others, one of the prophets." Talk is something less than what you know or believe in your own soul. You don't have to believe it because it's general; it can be attributed to someone else, as the question indicates. "Who do people say that I am?" Who do the townspeople, the boat people, the people by the sea, who do people say that I am? Jesus was asking, "What's the talk?"

Talk, you see, is indeed what you have heard. It is often unsubstantiated musings. It is speculative, often spurious smatterings of something you heard or thought you heard. Surety is not an issue, and conviction is not a prerequisite. Talk! "Who do people say that I am?" Some say John the Baptist, the forerunner, the one who eats locusts and wild honey.

This question is a prelude to the more important and personal question, "Who do you say that I am?" This second question demands a fearless faith that will culminate in a journey from mere talk to transforming testimony—testimony that requires faith, commitment, and conviction! Testimony is evidence given by a witness primarily to the action and requirements of God. Testimony is what someone says about the revelation of God in Jesus Christ. Testimony is your own word and deed about how God reveals God's self to those who are witnesses to God's power and truth.

Jesus knows something about testimony because Christ himself "bears testimony to God's work," but his testimony is often rejected. Come listen to Jesus as he testifies in the Gospel of John 3:11–13: "Very truly, I tell you, we speak of what we know and testify to what we have seen; yet you do not receive our testimony. If I have told you about earthly things and you do not believe, how can you believe if I tell you about heavenly things? No one has ascended into heaven except the one who descended from heaven, the Son of Man" (NRSV). Jesus does testify: "For God so loved the world that he gave his only Son, so that everyone who believes in him may not perish but may have eternal life" (John 3:16, NRSV). Peter's confession, "You are the Messiah" (Mark 8:29), is testimony from his faith and conviction. Testimony is particular; testimony is specific; testimony is grounded in your experience with Jesus as Lord and Savior. Testimony is based on your relationship with Jesus; testimony is one of the ways the Christian church came into being. People testify about their relationship with Jesus. Matthew writes his testimony. Mark's story of the gospel is his testimony. Luke, the physician, testifies. Peter and John had no silver and gold, but to the man at the gate, they say, "In the name of Jesus, get up and walk." Talk is general, but testimony is specific. Talk is devoid of commitment. Talk comes from the mind and the mouth. Testimony comes from searching the salient sayings of the soul buoyed by the power of the Holy Spirit.

John's disciples called him Rabbi, and he was a rabbi, a teacher, but not the Messiah. John is the forerunner, the preparer. John is not the bridegroom. The bridegroom has the bride, but John is just a friend of the bridegroom. He's a good man or maybe even the best man, but he's not the bridegroom. "Some say you are John the Baptist." They could remember John. They felt that John and Jesus sounded very much alike. This is the talk! Aha! He's John the Baptist—a dead man come back to life. "Some say you are John!"

And then some say he's Elijah, who according to the tradition and expectation was to return before the end of the age. Some say Elijah because they believe that anybody who preached that the kingdom of God was near must be Elijah. Some say Elijah, the great prophet praying unto the Lord and calling upon God to show his power against Ahab and Baal at the top of Mount Carmel. Elijah, the one who mocked the prophets of Baal as they called him to bring down fire.

Some say one of the prophets, but they know not which one. A prophet, you see, channels the word of the Lord, not the word of another prophet! So, you see it would be strange for Jesus to be a prophet in that sense because He wouldn't come to repeat just what the prophet Isaiah had to say, or the prophet Jeremiah, or Ezekiel, or Hosea, Joel, or Obadiah. Oh, he may have reminded them of one of the prophets, Jonah, Micah, Nahum, Habakkuk, Zephaniah, Haggai, Zechariah, or Malachi. But, my brothers and my sisters, Jesus is more than a prophet, greater than Moses and Micah, and more powerful than Daniel, Joshua, or Ezekiel.

After we shall have heard the testimonies of our slave foreparents, after the cries and prayers of Richard Allen and Absalom Jones, and the testimonies of Jarena Lee and Peter Williams and David Walker—after the testimonies of Sojourner Truth, Frederick Douglass, Paul Laurence Dunbar, W. E. B. Du Bois, Clara Thompson, James Weldon Johnson, Howard Thurman, Martin Luther King Jr., and the unnamed grandmothers and grandfathers, aunts and uncles of our families, who have prayed and testified about how good God is—then, my brothers and sisters, we too should have a testimony. I am blessed by the testimony of the saints. I'm blessed by the testimony of the seers and sages and the sober sayings of those who sing and shout, those whose limbs are no longer lame but limber, enabling them to leap and shout for joy.

I could talk to you about St. Augustine's *Confessions* or about Plato's *Republic* or Dante's *Inferno*. I could talk to you about urban America, about the issues facing our people. I could talk to you about urban education and higher education, about Christopher Jencks, John Goolad, about Sarah Lightfoot and Black church and what we ought to be doing, about deacons' and trustees' duties and responsibilities. I can talk to you about budgets and strategic plans, about youth and adults, about music and melody. I can talk to you about John the Baptist, about Elijah, about Paul and Timothy, but that is not why I decided to come here today. I came here not to talk, but to testify. To tell you how good God is, how God made me with his own hands, how God shaped me as the potter shapes the clay. I came by to say that talk is OK, but testimonies will win folks to Jesus. Talk may teach and tell, but testimony will transform your mind, body, and soul.

Can I testify? Can I testify about how the Lord woke me up this morning with the activity of my limbs, how he put food on my table and clothes on my back? Can I testify about the love of God when people say all kinds of evil and unfair judgments against me? God wraps his loving, comforting arms around me. Can I testify about how far the Lord has brought me? Can I testify about the sweet aroma of the gospel, this gospel that saved me from sin and self?

3

The Sermon as Interpretation

It has always been the responsibility of the church to broaden
horizons and challenge the status quo.
—Martin Luther King Jr., *Strength to Love*

Every week throughout the world, hundreds of thousands of
sermons are written and spoken to congregations of all
faiths and religious persuasions. In many ways, the sermon is
a poetic creation, an amalgamation of interpretation and
imagination culminating in the spoken word. It is also often,
but not always, grounded in an understanding of faith and a
written text vis-à-vis a community of faith—the congregation.
All of the elements or ingredients in the sermon must be interpreted, and this interpretation is then spoken to an interpreting
community. Thus, everything about sermonic discourse is
grounded in interpretation, and interpretation is grounded in
understanding. Moreover, the spokenness of African American
preaching has a dialogical character such that the voices of the
sermon are tantamount to what Mikhail Bakhtin calls *heteroglossia*. These many voices often rise from the scriptural
text, the preacher as text (a postmodern notion), the congregation as text, and the sermon itself as text.

So, the sermon, like the text and the congregation, is in fact
an "interpretation of an interpretation," as the late homiletician

Miles Jerome Jones would say. All written and spoken discourse is interpretation, even when it claims to be original. The sermon is like a novel, as described by Bakhtin:

> The novel can be defined as a diversity of social speech types (sometimes even diversity of languages) and a diversity of individual voices, artistically organized . . . These distinctive links and interrelationship between utterance and languages and speech types, its dispersion into the rivulets and droplets of social heteroglossia, its dialogization—this is the basic distinguishing feature of the stylistics of the novel.[1]

Inasmuch as the sermon, especially in the Black-church tradition, is a dialogical enterprise, it too is stylistically novelistic, especially in its spokenness. And in many ways, the sermon is not a sermon until it is spoken. It is written to be spoken more than read. Accordingly, in the African American church tradition, the congregation expects the preacher to speak as if he or she is speaking from an orality grounded in memory rather than in written discourse. Written discourse has to be written in a way that, when spoken, captures a natural rhythm and cadence that allows for dialogue. A person such as Martin Luther King Jr. was a master of the orality of the Black preacher. King represented the paradigm of Black theology, rhetoric, and orality; however, the Black preacher as a professional class of individuals has mastered this medium whether speaking extemporaneously or from a written manuscript.

In this chapter I search for the adequate hermeneutical framework to capture the dialogical character of black preaching, the need to see the multivalence of the scriptural and sermonic text, the deep symbolic meaning of the "word," and the ways in which the moral and relational dynamics of the sermon are revealed when we see its many similarities to a novel.

The Polyvalence of the Sermon

Every sermon is an interpretation of a text but also of its context and presuppositions in written or unwritten form. Further, adding to the interpretive polyphone, the preacher often does not know how the sermon is going to be interpreted by the hearer. Traditional white theologians have presumed interpretive authority such that a text means this or that—nothing more and nothing less. This is the straitjacket approach to meaning and interpretation. African American preaching, however, is creative and imaginative—fusing and finding your voice in the text amid all the other voices that are integral to the text. Meaning is often determined by the preacher/interpreter and the hearer/interpreter in dialogue with each other based on the context. The African American preacher is open to the multiplicity of voices that emanate from and surround the scripture text as well as the congregation and the society, which can also be "read" as "texts."

The language of the African American preacher—a language that extols freedom, justice, repentance, and salvation—is similarly multivoiced. It is often the language of the scriptural text as well as the language of the people and their contexts. It is a language of life and death, faith and hope. It is a language of freedom while yet struggling to be free. This is the language that Martin Luther King Jr. spoke in his speeches and sermons. It was a language that captured my spirit and spoke to my heart and soul. It was the language of Henry David Thoreau, Paul Tillich, Karl Barth, and Reinhold Niebuhr, as well as the language of Deacon Jones and Aunt Jane. It was a language that fused the experiences of the Black church and the white academy.

The Deep Symbolism of Plain Words

Interpreting the word and making the word plain involve the use of language, and language is no more than a symbol for understanding and clarification. Preaching, by its very nature, is laden with symbolism regarding grace, redemption, freedom, truth, and other principles. Moreover, the preacher's use of words, when spoken, constitutes the most effective symbolic reference of the sermon. The uttered, spoken word has new meaning each time it is spoken. This means that the sermon is never the same, even if the written words are the same, because each time the words are spoken, they create a new message by the nature of their meaning and sound. The philosopher Alfred North Whitehead states:

> A single word is not one definite sound. Every instance of its utterance differs in some respect from every other instance: the pitch of the voice, the intonation, the accent, the quality of the sound, the rhythmic relations of the component sounds, the intensity of sound all vary. Thus a word is a species of sounds, with specific identity and individual differences. When we recognize the species, we have heard the word. But what we have heard is merely the sound—euphonious or harsh, concordant with or discordant with other accompanying sounds. The word is heard in the pure perceptive mode of immediacy.[2]

This means that not only is the uttered instance of the word creating new meaning, but the word itself is different each time it is uttered. It sounds different and is therefore internalized differently by the hearer as well as the preacher. As symbols, words engender reflection and thought, causing the hearer to use other words that create connections between the words used by the preacher and the words these preached words have given rise to. Paul Ricoeur's notion that the "symbol gives rise to thought"[3] certainly reflects the inherent power of words.

The word is made plain by the symbolic reference of the word—the preached word. The word as symbol connects cause and effect, past and present, thought and feeling, the real and the ideal, and specifically in preaching, faith and praxis. Ultimately, this word is the interplay between life and death. Historically, the Black preacher, whether John Jasper or Henry Highland Garnett, has been able to use words to paint a picture with vivid clarity. The word as symbol of freedom was embodied by the preacher who spoke a word of hope to the congregation.

Symbolic reference is the interplay between two modes of perception, what Whitehead calls "causal efficacy and presentational immediacy."[4] Adapting his terms to sermonic points, presentational immediacy refers to the peripheral and initial understanding of a point. Thus, presentational immediacy is the preacher's ability to interpret the language of the text in a way that he or she immediately perceives to be true and relevant. Causal efficacy, on the other hand, as it relates to point development, has to do with what is behind the initial description of the point. What is the basis of the assertion being made, and how did the preacher arrive at such an assertion?

The preacher is in a precarious position. When the text appears to be and is in fact simple, the preacher is compelled to delve deeper into it such that he or she is able to squeeze, milk, and tease out of the text more than the hearers could ever imagine on their own accord. This is when the preacher shows what she or he is really made of. This is the time to use the preacher's knowledge of history, literature, philosophy, art, anthropology, education, psychology, theology, interpretation theory, languages, linguistics, biblical studies, and other arts and sciences. A simple statement such as "Jesus wept" offers itself to be interpreted and expounded upon in ways that make use of Christology, incarnation, anthropology, biology, psychology, etc. It is the preacher's responsibility to explain and to make rich and resonant that which on the surface appeared to be easy and simple.

Conversely, the preacher is compelled to simplify that which is complex and convoluted. For example, some passages in Paul's letter to the Romans seem to be laden with thickness and complexity. He states, "Welcome all the Lord's followers, even those whose faith is weak. Don't criticize them for having beliefs that are different from yours" (Romans 14:1, CEV; also see Romans 14:3–11 or Romans 14:14–15:3). Paul's contrast of the weak and the strong leads the preacher to understand first who constitute the weak and the strong in Rome and what is the relationship between the weak and the "stumbling," and so on. What is the relationship between the "weak" and the "strong" and Christianity and Judaism?[5] These questions need to be answered, and the complex issues in texts like these need to be simplified.

Finally, most people in the congregation are seeking ways to make real that which has been preached. This means that the preacher must make the Word "portable" as Dr. Sam Proctor would say, or "applicable," as my colleague Nathan Dell encourages. People really do want to be able to apply the message to their everyday lives. To do this, they need from the preacher a clear example of how folk in the pews can apply a complex or simple idea to their lives. This is not always easy to achieve, but the preacher must make the effort to help people understand how this truth, this principle, this moral, or this teaching applies to them in their current condition. How can I actually love my enemies, or how can I really forgive someone who has blatantly wronged me?

Applying the text requires that the preacher be creative and imaginative in his or her approach to textual development because imagination has within it the inherent ability to reflect the image of God (*imago Dei*) as Creator. In imagination, the preacher is constantly creating a new world, a new reality, a new being—making the impossible possible. This is exactly what the African American preacher has been practicing from the days of slavery to this very present age. Application and imagination go hand in hand.

Textuality and Dialogue Preaching

An expansive and suggestive framework for thinking about dialogical character of the sermon is Mikhail M. Bakhtin's *Dialogical Imagination*. Specifically, his chapter "Discourse in the Novel" contains a potpourri of themes, features, and concepts that are crucial to the interpretation process. I am drawn to his concepts of style and meaning, understanding and response of the listener, the limitations of poetry, and the presence of other voices in our speech and writing.

Some things that Bakhtin says resonate in the African American preaching tradition because style is so crucial to African American life and preaching. Bakhtin makes it clear that the utterance—that is, the word—is socially constituted. It is not uttered in a vacuum but in a world where there is love, hate, war, peace, justice, and injustice. The semantic and axiological nature of utterance is evident; in other words, the meaning of the language and the universally recognized truth of the word is clear. The unity of form and substance is made clear from the start. He states, "Form and content in discourse are one, once we understand that verbal discourse is a social phenomenon—social throughout its entire range and in each and every [one] of its factors, from the sound image to the furtherest reaches of abstract meaning."[6] This verbal discourse is the word, which is as microscopic as "thanks," "Amen," or "O God" and as lengthy as a sermon, poem, or novel.

The social tone of the utterance is critical to the stylistics of the genre. Bakhtin argues that in fact all discourse is a socially constructed phenomenon. He states, "But these individual and tendentious overtones of style, cut off from the fundamentally social modes in which discourse lives, inevitably come across as flat and abstract in such a formulation and cannot therefore be studied in organic unity with a work's semantic components."[7]

Consider how this applies to other genres, the novel and the poem. The novel, by its nature and style, is laden with heteroglossia, or many voices. It is diverse and full of voices, experiences, and languages. Bakhtin states that diversity and sociality are integral to the typology:

> The novel can be defined as a diversity of social speech types (sometimes even diversity of languages) and a diversity of individual voices artistically organized. The internal stratification of any single national language into social dialects, characteristic group behavior, professional jargons, generic languages, languages of generations and age groups, tendentious languages, languages of the authorities, of various circles and of passing fashions, languages that serve the specific sociopolitical purposes of the day, even of the hour (each day has its own slogan, its own vocabulary, its own emphases)— this internal stratification present in every language at any given moment of its historical existence is the indispensable prerequisite for the novel as a genre.[8]

Clearly, the novel is constituted by the speech of many voices. One voice is not an option. One never speaks with one voice, because our voices are inhibited and inhabited by other voices. Nevertheless, for Bakhtin, heteroglossia is always the reality, even when we are unaware of it. The voices of the many are integral to our speech—the past, the present, the beautiful, and the ugly are all making utterances!

Bakhtin suspects that, unlike discourse in the novel, poetry tries to give language too much order, thereby making language single-voiced. He makes this point clear when he states:

> But—we repeat—in the majority of poetic genres, the unity of the language system and the unity (and uniqueness) of the poet's individuality as reflected in his language and speech, which is directly realized in this unity, are indispensable prerequisites of poetic style. The novel, however, not only does not require these conditions but (as we have said) even makes of the internal stratification of language, of its social heteroglossia and the variety of individual voices in it, the prerequisite for authentic novelistic prose.[9]

Is the preacher, then, like the singer or the rapper, more like a single-voiced artist or one who speaks with many voices—a heteroglot? Is the preacher more like a novelist or a poet? Is the sermon more like a poem or a novel? Or is it fair to say, as Bakhtin does, that the individuality of the poet's language or speech is constitutive of one voice?

Historically, the African American preacher has spoken with many voices while remaining a poet. I think Martin Luther King Jr. was a good example of "dialogized heteroglossia" while simultaneously remaining a poet. He certainly played the voice of reason, exemplified by his interest in philosophers and theologians like Immanuel Kant, G. W. F. Hegel, and Paul Tillich, against the voices of white segregationists and the white church. King embodied the semantic and the symbiotic nature of the meaning of poetry and prose. Likewise, some rap artists, poets like Tupac Shakur, were able to do the same through musical lyrics. In African American preaching, there is a nexus between the novelistic and the poetic.

Understanding and Response

Another element of dialogue in Bakhtin is related to understanding, and that is response. He suggests that understanding is grounded in response. The speaker depends on some type of response from the hearer to validate understanding. Bakhtin states, "Understanding comes to fruition only in the response. Understanding and response are dialectically merged and mutually condition each other; one is impossible without the other."[10] This dialogue between speaker and listener has characterized the majority of African American preaching such that one has informed the other.

The preacher must be oriented toward the listener if understanding and faith development are to be achieved. Bakhtin states:

> It is precisely such an understanding that the speaker counts on. Therefore his orientation toward the listener is an orientation toward a specific conceptual horizon, toward the specific world of the listener; it introduces totally new elements into his discourse; it is a way, after all that various different points of view, conceptual horizons, systems for providing expressive accents, various social "languages" come to interact with one another. "The speaker strives to get a reading on his own word, and on his own conceptual system that determines this word, within the alien conceptual system of the understanding receiver; he enters into a dialogical relationship with certain aspects of this system."[11]

This suggests that the speaker has to deconstruct the social context or, more precisely, interpret the context and the listener in order to foster understanding. Understanding is active and process-oriented such that there can be no disinterested discourse if the goal is understanding and clarity rather than self-aggrandizement. "The word lives, as it were, on the boundary between its own context and another, alien, context."[12]

In reference specifically to preaching, I wonder if the church may not be an alien context for the word, especially if that word elicits no response. This may mean that there is a disconnect between the preacher and the listener or that the power and presence of heteroglossia in both the preacher and listener are drowning out or canceling both voices. The voices of the many, when played against each other, can either advance or destroy the voice of the poet as the preacher. It is a difficult and dangerous discourse that has to be dialogical if understanding is to be achieved. Mikhail Bakhtin helps in so many ways because his thoughts intersect with so many other disciplines, especially those that are word-oriented, such as preaching and poetics.

Additionally, let us bring other voices into the discussion. According to Jacques Derrida, writing is a supplement and to some extent a replacement for speech. Moreover, there is something about Derrida's *Monolingualism of the Other* that confounds and intrigues at the same time. The universal assertion endemic to Derrida that seems to permeate every page of *Monolingualism* is this: "Yes, I only have one language, yet it is not mine."[13] He puts it another way as a double law in the very next chapter:

1. We only ever speak one language or rather one idiom.
2. We never speak only one language, or rather there is no idiom.[14]

He later states, "Consequently, anyone should be able to declare under oath: I have only one language and it is not mine; my language is, for me, a language that cannot be assimilated. My language, the only one I hear myself speak and agree to speak, is the language of the other."[15] This means that my own voice is not mine, yet it is mine. It belongs to the other and to me because I am the other.

This is a fusion of Derrida, who speaks in a double voice, creating and to some extent overcoming dichotomies very much like the style-and-substance or content-and-form correlations of Martha Nussbaum. Nussbaum asserts that there is an intimate connection between form and content. Emotion is a critical component of discourse, as is Kantian reason. Western philosophy has regained the "form" component of the alliance between form and content, as Nussbaum asserts. In her philosophical hermeneutics, feeling is very important; feelings, emotions, and the affective contribute to understanding and ontology. In response to Descartes's *"Cogito ergo sum,"* Nussbaum and Friedrich Schleiermacher could say with some degree of ease, "I feel; therefore, I am." This does not obviate thinking; however, it places emotions on a positive footing or at least acknowledges the critical importance of feeling as an existential reality. Nussbaum states:

> There is, with respect to any text carefully written and fully imagined, an organic connection between its form and its content. Certain thoughts and ideas, a certain sense of life, reach toward expression in writing that has a certain shape and form, that uses certain structures, certain terms. Just as the plant emerges from the seeded soil, so the novel and its terms flower from and express the conceptions of the author, his or her sense of what matters. If the writing is well done, a paraphrase in a very different form and style will not in general, express the same conception.[16]

Subject matter is integrally subjective, and the form it takes emanates from the subject both as writer and as what is written. This feeling and style is expressive of life—what is important and what is not. Nussbaum says, "Life is never simply presented by a text; it is always *represented* as something."[17] The connection between feeling and thinking is a legitimate one that is often lacking in Anglo-American philosophy and in other discourse. Style that can be equated with feeling has been dismissed by philosophy, yet Nussbaum asserts, "I wish to establish the importance of taking style seriously in its expressive and statement making functions."[18] For Nussbaum, the text is speaking to the reader, the writer, and the other. One cannot extricate himself or herself from the life of the text, nor can one detach the text from life. There is an ethical and moral relationship among the novel, the story (that is, the text), and the reader. This connection, when properly made by the preacher, constitutes the dialogic nature of the preached word.

Relationality between reader and the text is evident throughout Nussbaum. For Nussbaum and Hans Georg Gadamer, the text is speaking to the reader. The plot of the story or novel has a moral quality that is as important as the actions themselves. For Nussbaum, the purpose of reading a novel is to engage in ethical inquiry so that one can understand more fully the Aristotelian question of ethics: how should one live? This question is a starting point or a prelude to the more important practical, ethical questions of life—questions about doing that which is fair, just, right, etc. Novel reading or certain literary texts are indispensable to ethical inquiry. Nussbaum writes double-voiced philosophical essays in the same way that the novel speaks and in a similar way that Derrida speaks.

I began by saying that Derrida speaks in a double voice: "I have but one language—yet that language is not mine." On one very deep level, I yearn to know and to speak my native language—a language erased from my memory by three hundred years of slavery and alienation. Both Charles Long and Anthony Pinn would agree that this erasure began during the

Middle Passage from the west coast of Africa and continued unabated on the auction blocks in Virginia, Georgia, the Carolinas, and so forth until the Civil Rights Act of 1964. This is reminiscent of what W. E. B. Du Bois called "double-consciousness"—an imposition of the "other," or a "seventh son, born with a veil." He writes:

> After the Egyptian and Indian, the Greek and Roman, the Teuton and Mongolian, the Negro is a sort of seventh son, born with a veil, and gifted with second sight in this American world—a world which yields him no true self-consciousness, but only lets him see himself through the revelation of the *other world.* It is a peculiar sensation, this double-consciousness, this sense of always looking at one's self through *the eyes of others,* of measuring one's soul by the tape of a world that looks on in amused contempt and pity. One even feels his twoness—An American, a Negro; two souls, two thoughts, two unreconciled strivings; two warring ideals in one dark body, whose dogged strength alone keeps it from being torn asunder.[19]

This description focuses on the influence of the "other" in creating a synthesized self in the African American. This pandemic, ubiquitous other that influences one's ontology has as one of its constituent elements language. "The eyes of others" is the monolingualism of the other, the speech and writing of the other—the Derridian merger of speech and language into a DuBoisian "double-consciousness" that ultimately is manifested in the monolingualism of the other, a type of hegemony of the soul. Derrida states, "This monolingualism of the other certainly has the threatening face and features of colonial hegemony."[20] This is the case because the monolingualist speaks a language that does not belong to him—a language of which he is deprived because one's own language is also the language of the other.

This is exactly how I interpret Du Bois's concept of "double-consciousness." It is a type of self-consciousness, and self-consciousness is in fact consciousness of the other.

Interpretation of Novels as a Hermeneutical Discipline

For preachers to become keen interpreters of life and other texts, the reading of novels is a necessary practice. The ethical or moral dilemma, the philosophy and cultural location embedded in the novel can provide an opportunity to interpret and understand real-life situations. Pieces such as Toni Morrison's *The Bluest Eye* or Ernest Gaines's *The Gathering of Old Men* contribute to our ontological, theological, and cultural understanding.

Two novels that provide an excellent vehicle for understanding metaphor, event/meaning, and other principles we have explored are *A Lesson before Dying* by Ernest Gaines and *Invisible Man* by Ralph Ellison. Both of these fictional discourses are quite classic in that they capture the *Geist* of the meaning of interpretation from a perspective that philosopher Enrique Dussel refers to as living on the periphery and what I have termed "the underside of culture."

Search for the Self in a Racist Context

In *A Lesson before Dying*, understanding is very much the same as it is for Hans Gadamer—an ontological phenomenon, that is, a part of being and recognizing that being also has negation. This negation of being is what Miles Jones describes as death. The opening lines in the book, "I was not there, yet I was there," speak of both Jefferson's trial and his crucifixion because Grant, the teacher and narrator, opted out of attending both events. The "not there-ness" is unable to cancel out the "being there" because being there had nothing to do with space and time but with the spirit of the existential situation and the fact that "not being there" was powerless in any effort to obviate being there. Being there and not being there are therefore not dichotomies but a part of the otherness of being. Moreover, this, like every statement, is a statement about the self, and every statement about the self is an intersection with otherness.

In *A Lesson before Dying,* the defense attorney (who was court-appointed) sought to get Jefferson, the wrongly accused yet presumed guilty African American, acquitted by referring to him as a "hog"—an ignorant, sloppy, unreflecting animal. The "defense" lawyer states:

> Gentlemen of the jury, look at this—this—this boy. I almost said man, but I can't say man. Oh sure, he has reached the age of twenty-one, when we, civilized men, consider the male species has reached manhood, but would you call this—this—this a man? No, not I. I would call it a boy and a fool. A fool is not aware of right and wrong. A fool does what others tell him to do. A fool got into that automobile. A man with a modicum of intelligence would have seen that those racketeers meant no good. But not a fool . . . Gentlemen of the jury, look at him—look at him—look at this. Do you see a man sitting here? Do you see a man sitting here? . . . Do you see a modicum of intelligence? Do you see anyone here who could plan a murder, a robbery, can plan—can plan—can plan anything? A cornered animal to strike quickly out of fear, a trait inherited from his ancestors in the deepest jungle of blackest Africa—yes, yes, that he can do—but to plan? To plan gentlemen, this skull here holds no plans. What you see there is a thing that acts on command. A thing to hold the handle of a plow, a thing to load your bales of cotton . . .[21]

The defense attorney continues on ad infinitum with his derogatory and excruciatingly demeaning and warped use of language, images, and metaphors until he concludes that he is not even defending a human being. After pleading for mercy and saying that his client, Jefferson, was in fact innocent of the charges of robbery and murder, the lawyer says, "But let us say he was not. Let us for a moment say he was not. What justice would there be to take this life? Justice, gentlemen? Why, I would just as soon put a *hog* in the electric chair as this."[22]

Jefferson was indeed found guilty of robbery and first-degree murder by a judge and jury of twelve white men, and a few days later was sentenced to death by electrocution. Miss Emma, Jefferson's godmother, sat through the trial but was not able to extirpate from her memory the ontological negation of Jefferson's humanity by his own defense attorney, who referred to him as a hog. One of the most enduring themes of the book is reflected in the thinking of Miss Emma as she communicates her concern to Grant, the professor. She states, "I know he was just trying to get him off. But they didn't pay that no mind. Still gave him death . . . I don't want them to kill no hog, she said. I want a man to walk to that chair, on his own two feet."[23]

This becomes the challenge for one of the central characters in the book—Grant, who was the teacher who hated teaching because he felt that he was not making any progress in that community. Nevertheless, Miss Emma wanted Grant to teach her godson Jefferson how to walk to that electric chair as a man and not as a hog, a metaphor or symbol for ignorance and nonbeing. The hog grunts and slouches in mud and meaninglessness very much represented in this story by the size and the antics of the superintendent of the school district.

This book is laden with double messages and heteroglossia. For example, Dr. Joseph, the superintendent, is satisfied and impressed with Grant's most intellectually challenged student:

"And he called on the one boy in class who I wished had stayed home today. He was without doubt the worst child in the school . . . Dr. Joseph asked his name, and he ran together three words even I couldn't understand. His name was Louis Washington, Jr., but what he said didn't sound anything like that."[24]

Grant, the teacher, often questioned himself about staying in that community and whether he was making an impact on the students. His constant questioning of himself is a question of being motivated by the same spirit that we glimpse in Ralph Ellison's novel *Invisible Man*, where the main character is in search of self. The most searing and poignant words of ontological understanding are found in the opening lines of the prologue:

> I am an invisible man. No, I am not a spook like those who haunted Edgar Allen Poe; nor am I one of your Hollywood-movie ectoplasms. I am a man of substance, of flesh and bone, fiber and liquids—And I might even be said to possess a mind. I am invisible, understand, simply because people refuse to see me. Like the bodiless heads you see sometimes in circus shows, it is as though I have been surrounded by mirrors of hard, distorting glass. When they approach me they see only my surroundings, themselves, or figments of their imagination—indeed, everything and anything except me.[25]

This seeing "everything and anything except me" is exactly the ontological negation that permeates *A Lesson before Dying*. It is felt by Grant, the teacher; by Jefferson, the death row inmate; by Miss Emma, Grant's aunt and friend Tante Lou, and Jefferson's godmother; and by the children in the classroom. They are all trying to be respected in a society and community that is grounded in racism, injustice, and the violation of human freedom and dignity.

Images of the Black Preacher

For the preacher, another novelistic theme that contributes to understanding and interpretation is the characterization of preachers. In particular, the self-understanding of the Black preacher includes the recognition that popular culture has often portrayed our role in a less than flattering light. *A Lesson before Dying* often portrays the preacher as a naive ignoramus—a simpleton who doesn't quite understand the complexities of life and whose beliefs are irrational and grounded in myth. The preacher in this novel is one of the most unlikable characters presented in stereotypical form. He is presented as the equivalent to Bakhtin's "fool" or "clown" in the novel. Bakhtin says, "Hypocrisy and falsehood saturate all human relationships."[26] If this is true, then the preacher is no exception, especially as he is presented in novels, television, and movies.

These elements of popular culture seem to portray the preacher in negative terms that resemble his image during slavery. H. Beecher Hicks, in his book *Images of the Black Preacher*, indicates that the slave preacher was a tool for controlling other slaves, often thought to be an ignorant opiate, a unifying force as well as an agent of protest. Hicks writes:

> In sum, the black preacher was seen by slave masters as a tool to be used to control the masses of slaves, as a parasite gouging life from his people for his own gain, an opium used for oppressive purposes, and as an ignorant buffoon felt to be incapable of delivering the gospel with any sense of authenticity or integrity. The collective force of this interpretation of the slave preacher's purpose and function has been maintained through biased historical accounts and overpopular folklore.[27]

Hicks proceeds by explaining the complex dialectic that the slave preacher embodied. What the white slave master construed and perceived one way, the black preacher interpreted and used in another way. Hicks explains:

> On the contrary, however, the slave preacher was able to turn his predicament into possibility. While the master used him as a tool, he took and used it to plow up fertile spiritual ground. What seemed to the master an amusing but inept homily was laced with lessons only the oppressed could comprehend. That opium the slave master would have used as a drug, the slave preacher converted to the sweet balm that made life bearable. Though clothed in the sheepskin of submission, he planted seeds of soul from which grew the inevitable plants of protest and rebellion.[28]

The African American preacher remains an enigma, a complex compilation of personality types and leadership styles. Yet those writers and filmmakers continue to portray him in terms that are more negative than positive—terms that are grounded more in myth and folklore than in truth and reality. Because the preacher speaks of high moral standards and biblical ideals, fiction writers tend to hyperbolize their description and depiction of the Black preacher. The preacher is often portrayed as an appetitive, verbose, styling, hustling, fast-talking, slick, manipulative individual. While there may be a few preachers who fit these stereotypical images, the overwhelming majority of preachers are quite honest, articulate, sincere, astute, compassionate, caring, and kind. However, these images do not sell books or movies and are seldom used to describe the Black preacher. Nevertheless, throughout America and the world, there are Black preachers who are transforming communities and lives on a regular basis. These are the unwritten (about) and the undocumented lives of those who preach. The unpopular preacher is indeed the best preacher.

The following sermon applies these principles of interpretation to a text from Ephesians. As you read, look for simplicity, complexity, and application of the words to daily life. Consider what voices are expressed and where the preacher might be engaged in a dialogue with the listeners. Finally, return to the sermon text, and consider what themes emerge for you, drawing on your own reading and experience, as you engage in dialogue with the writer of this epistle.

Sermon *The Power of God*

> I ask that your minds may be opened to see his light, so that you will know what is the hope to which he has called you, how rich are the wonderful blessings he promises his people, and how very great is his power at work in us who believe. This power working in us is the same as the mighty strength which he used when he raised Christ from death and seated him at his right side in the heavenly world. Christ rules there above all heavenly rulers, authorities, powers, and lords; he has a title superior to all titles of authority in this world and in the next. God put all things under Christ's feet and gave him to the church as supreme Lord over all things. The church is Christ's body, the completion of him who himself completes all things everywhere.
> —Ephesians 1:18–23, TEV

Power and powerlessness are often perceived as opposites. But I believe that powerlessness is an inherent component of any earthly power. When we look at ourselves fully, we see that inherent in our quest for power is powerlessness. For example, political power is intimately tied to the "will" of the people. We can have guns and missiles, tanks and ships, but if the heart and soul of the people desire *peace* and *not violence*, then our political leaders are powerless. There is something within us all that is lured by power—whether it is money, influence, position, intelligence, experience, physical strength, or whatever, we are obsessed with the desire for power—whether it's the power of the military, industry, business, the media, etc. Everybody wants power, and the powerless—whether they are the poor, the disenfranchised, the weak, the young, or the old—they too want to be empowered; they want the clout, the influence to set the agenda and to determine their own destiny.

In this country we often hear the media describe the president as the most powerful leader of the free world. The power of the presidency is discussed and debated by us all. Indeed, it is relative because in human terms, whatever power we have is really so tenuous, so temporary, so momentary, it is almost whimsical. Whatever power we have is bestowed on us by the vote of the majority or by some entity that has the right to determine the influence and strength of another.

As a child, I remember thinking that my daddy was the strongest, most powerful man on earth because he could lift heavy objects, carry two of us on his shoulders, and instill fear in all of us. And then one day my father "took sick" in the middle of the night. He had a heart attack, and I saw him on a stretcher, in the hospital—lying prostrate—unable to stand and care for himself. And I realized the transitoriness of my father's strength and power. I realized that there was an element of weakness and powerlessness even in his strength. A man who was physically strong, who was constitutionally strong—one who in my world represented stability and power—one who could speak to any of us and demand compliance and respect, one whose word was law, was now weakened by the deterioration of his heart. This experience forced me to come to grips with the powerlessness of the human mind and body, on one hand, and the absolute power of God, on the other. The only thing that we could do was pray to God, and God heard and answered our prayer, and my father returned home to live, because God spared him for thirteen more years.

God Is a God of Power. Unlike those of us who often think that we possess some kind of power—whether it's over individuals, organizations, or communities—our perceived power is in essence weakness in disguise, weakness masquerading often as egocentrism, weakness disguised as strength and might. Our power is often tied to politics and economics. This power is very necessary and important to government, but we need something more eternal, something more everlasting, something more encompassing, something that embraces all of God's creation. We need something that is essential to our very life! The power we need cannot be contained or restrained; this power cannot be bought or sold; this power cannot be exchanged or traded. This power cannot be manipulated, compromised, or coerced! This power is the Power of God. It is inherent to the nature of God. In other words, God is power—you cannot say the word *God* without implying power. God, the word *God* necessitates power; God, the word *God* is indicative of power. When you say "God," you give power a new meaning.

There is nothing transitory or tenuous, nothing latent or limiting, nothing restraining or restrictive about the power of God. Unlike the power of Rome with her gladiators and symbols of oppression and corruption, God's power is a loving, self-giving power! Paul's prayer for the Ephesians was that they might know how powerful God is. He wanted them to fully grasp, to be totally enlightened about the power of God. Now we ask, "How are we to understand the power of God? What makes the power of God so unique—so different than all other forms of power?"

First, for the believer, God's power is so great that it cannot be measured. The power of God is believer's power. The text says, "How very great is his power at work in us who believe." This power of God is spiritual power, the ability to achieve peace in the midst of chaos and confusion. Indeed, while Rome had peace brought on by the power of the sword, while civilization flourished from a distance, there was slavery, violence, and cruelty within her gates. It was a powerful province, but it was held in bondage by its own earthly power—its mighty armies, its warped sense of justice. To this very world, Paul prays that God's power is so great that it cannot be measured. In the midst of all this display of might and worldly power, Paul says that the believer is empowered by God—not by political might, not by sword, not by the flesh, not by violence, but by God. For the believer, *God is Power!*

Second, the power of God working in us is resurrection power. This power of God exceeds our grandest ideas or understanding of power. This means that the power of God working in us is able to transform death into life. The text states, "This power working in us is the same as the mighty strength which he used when he raised Christ from death and seated him at his right side in the heavenly world." The power of God working in us is strong enough to defy nature and even destroy the last enemy, which is death. This power to overcome death and to lift up Jesus and seat him at the right side of God—this is the power of God! It is the power that can bring to life the death in us. Whether it is a Kierkegaardian hopelessness, fear, or despair; whether it's a decaying spirit or a decadent mind; whether it is the dreams of a child or parent, dashed by drugs or depression, we do have the power in us to overcome. This resurrection power, this mighty strength that raised up Jesus after he had been beaten, brutalized, and flogged—crucified and died, this mighty power of God raised him up—God, the great omnipotent One, God who clothes the grass in green and enables the sparrow to sing, God who "sits high and looks low" is the ultimate meaning of power.

If I could humanize and contextualize the God that I know, the One who, in the language of our forefathers, "woke me up this morning and started me on my way," the one who gave me strength throughout the day, then I would say that God has more power in his little finger than all of the armies of the earth. I would say that God is a good God. God is Powerful! God is so wide, you can't get around him, so tall you can't get over him . . . *God is Power!* For he created the earth, the stars, and the moon; he sends rain upon the just and the unjust—and he transforms death to life. He did not simply *raise* Jesus Christ, but he *raised him up and* set him on the right side of the Father. That's the *Power of God!*

Finally, the power of God manifests itself in the empowerment of the powerless. Jesus Christ's death, resurrection, and ascension reflect how the one who was perceived as a paradigm of powerlessness is now the pinnacle of power. Jesus Christ as symbol for those who are placed last, the downtrodden, the suffering, the crucified has now become exalted (lifted up). He is now the essential enigmatic essence of the power of God. The text says, "Christ rules there above all heavenly rulers, authorities, powers, and lords; he has a title superior to all titles of authority in this world and in the next. God put all things under Christ's feet and gave him to the church as supreme Lord over all things. The church is Christ's body, the completion of him who himself completes all things everywhere" (verses 21–23). The exalted Christ is Lord of all. The one who was despised and rejected, spat upon, and pierced in the side; the one who was ostracized, mimicked, mocked, and muted by the taunts of the religious authorities and the crowds; the one who was challenged and ridiculed by scribes and Pharisees alike, denied and "dissed" by his own disciples. The one who was castigated, mutilated, emasculated, and rejected earlier by Saul is now, in the words of Paul, the transformed Hebrew of Hebrews, this Jesus is now ruler above all heavenly angels. His title is above all titles. Everything—all things—have been put under his feet. The same Jesus who was crucified is now exalted! The church in the power of Christ is a church united with him in power and might! The church, in the language of Jürgen Moltmann, is now a church in the "power of the Holy Spirit," the body of Christ revitalized, revived, renewed, and reborn—all because of the power of the Almighty God.

4

The Sermon as Art

When art dresses itself in the most worn-out material it is
most easily recognized as art.
—Friedrich Nietzsche

Style is a factor in the person to person encounter at which
preaching aims.
—Robert J. McCracken

Preaching is by its nature an acoustical event, having its home
in orality not textuality.
—Fred B. Craddock

To speak of power is to speak of something other than
"speech" even if the power of speaking is thereby implied. It is
a power that does not pass over completely into articulation
since it is the experience of efficacy par excellence.
—Paul Ricoeur

Preaching style is not the antithesis of content but a corollary
or constituent element of the content and hermeneutics
(theory) of preaching. If the task of hermeneutics is to bridge the
distance between text and interpreter (or listener), the orality
and gestures of the preacher often contribute to the effectiveness
of preaching. The expressions of the preacher, verbal and non-
verbal, are a part of the worship in the community of faith. Walter Ong asserts, "Some non-oral communication is exceedingly

rich—gesture, for example. Yet in a deep sense language, articulated sound, is paramount. Not only communication, but thought itself relates in an altogether special way to sound."[1]

In African American preaching, the sound of the trumpet—the voice—is a critical component of the communication process. I have heard hundreds of churchgoers after listening to the preacher on Sunday morning make comments like "He really sounds good" or "I like the way he sounds" or "He really preached today!" When they are pressed as to the meaning of such terminology or if asked what the sermon was about, it is not unusual to get a response like "I don't really know what the subject was nor the scripture reference, but he surely did *sound* good to me; he or she really preached." This suggests that the nexus between the oral and the aural is always a part of the existential present and contributes to the meaning of the message in the mind of the hearer. The spoken word has power; what you hear is indeed what you get. This means that African American preaching is often as acoustical as it is semantic.

The style of the Black preacher has a sociopolitical component as well. By this I mean that style is an expression of freedom and liberation. Preaching, simply by being done by persons who historically were enslaved, is in essence a subversive act and may represent a true and authentic Africanism.

Black preachers and parishioners understand the nature of homiletics and recognize that style without substance is typically more acceptable than substance without style. Quite frankly, substance without style is more often than not dead on arrival! However, in Black preaching, there is no true dichotomy between substance and style; rather, there is a nexus between the two.

Beyond the Limits of Reason Alone

Black preaching has always been an amalgamation of reason and feeling, or rationality and emotions. It is much more of a holistic enterprise than reason alone. This does not mean that it is without reason. It is just not restrained or limited by reason, nor does it concentrate on a supposed autonomous human will. The words of Paul are helpful in illuminating our understanding and practice of preaching. He writes, "My speech and my proclamation were not with plausible words of wisdom, but with a *demonstration of the Spirit and of power*, so that your faith might rest not on human wisdom but on the power of God" (1 Corinthians 2:4–5, NRSV, italics added).

The African American poet laureate Langston Hughes captures the spirit of Black preaching in his poem "Prayer":

> I ask you this:
> Which way to go?
> I ask you this:
> Which sin to bear?
> Which crown to put
> Upon my hair?
> I do not know,
> Lord God,
> I do not know.[2]

Human destiny is not determined by one's own reason or will but by a higher power, as Langston Hughes suggests. We are not autonomous beings. While reason is a critical component of our nature, it is not to be deified. When rationalism elevates human reason to the place of supreme authority and makes Jesus an archetype or a construct of reason, this is contrary to slave religion and Black theology, which are heavily dependent on the power of God to transform evil individuals and structures and turn the world "upside down" and "inside out." African American preaching, then, is not constrained by reason or rationality but reflects the limits of reason and the power of the spirit. It is really a holistic enterprise—an amalgam of body, soul, and spirit that manifests itself to a large degree in orality and gesturality.

The gestures of the body, particularly the hands, are rational expressions of the meaning and power of God. The preacher is an acting being inasmuch as the gesture is a movement of the body designed to communicate meaning. Gestures, then, are as rational as they are emotive; therefore, they convey meaning. Historically, the hands have played a prominent role in Christian rhetoric or preaching. Moreover, the classical Greek and Roman philosophers recognized the importance of hand gestures as expressions of knowledge and meaning. Gesture often means hand movement or that the hands are the tools of rationality. Aristotle says, "Man has hands because he is the wisest of all beings." The hands and feet are the most prominent indicators of the body's creative motion. "There is style or strategy in the rhythm of human body movement. This measured motion is intimately connected with speech (verbal gesture). It is thus a rational activity. Repetition is the law that guides the rhythm of human gesture."[3]

W. E. B. Du Bois, in *The Souls of Black Folk*, maintains that the Black preacher represents a continuous lineage of the influence of Africa on American soil. In many ways, E. Franklin Frazier, the noted African American sociologist, makes the same point but draws a different conclusion, often vacillating between accepting and not accepting the role of Africa in the religious and social development of the "Negro" preacher and the "Negro" church in America. The slave preacher could raise his voice, holler, and move his limbs in a way that represented a freedom not experienced by others who fell under the oppressive and controlling hand of the master. The preacher could give voice to the power of the Holy Spirit not subject to the control of any person. The act of preaching became the embodiment of meaning and being. This means that orality and gesturality became an embodied hermeneutic. Albert J. Raboteau says:

> The presence of God became manifest in the words, the gestures, and the bodily movements of the believers . . . in this

ecstatic form of African American worship, the divine was
embodied in the faithful. The emotional ecstasy of the
slaves' worship services conveyed their belief that the whole
human person—body as well as spirit—made God present
and so the human person became an image of God.[4]

The orality and gesturality of the African American
preacher have their roots in Africa and in the "invisible institution" of the antebellum South, where Black slaves secretly
practiced their religion out of the presence of whites. The slave
preacher was a leader of this "invisible institution" and learned
to speak in a language that had a double meaning of freedom
in this world and the next. "Slave preachers led the meetings
of the 'invisible institution' and exercised a good deal of influence among the slaves in general. Although most were illiter-
ate, their verbal artistry earned the slave preachers the respect
of blacks and sometimes whites as well. . . . Many slave
preachers practiced a style of revivalistic preaching that has
come to be called the chanted sermon because of its rhythmic
structure and musical tone."[5]

Nommo and Kuntu:
Word and Style in Preaching

Nommo means the magical power of the word, that is, the life
force that emanates from the word, and *Kuntu* has to do with
the immutability of style in African culture. It is a "mode of
existence [*Kuntu*] which is determined by meaning and
rhythm."[6] These two elements, word and rhythm, are integral
to Black preaching style or the aesthetics of preaching. The
Black preacher takes a word, a simple word, and plays with its
parts—using prefixes and suffixes, elongating its syllables, and
repeating it time and time again, creating a new poetry, a new
rhythm to its sound, and often a new meaning. Meaning and
rhythm are interconnected, bound together in Black preaching

like "white on rice" or as "sweetness is to honey." African philosopher Janheinz Jahn states in his book *Muntu*, "In every concrete expression of this culture meaning and rhythm are inseparably interwoven."[7]

Anyone who has grown up in the traditional Black church has witnessed and experienced the cultural rhythms of the preachers and the poets. Almost all recitations are done with emphatic expression, a rhythmic cadence born out of the sound of the drum and percussive beats of Africa. Jahn makes this clearer by referring to Léopold Sédar Senghor's definition of rhythm as "the architecture of being, the dynamic that gives it form, the pure expression of the life force." Jahn continues:

> Rhythm is the vibrating shock, the force which, through our sense, grips us at the root of our being. It is expressed through corporeal and sensual means; through . . . accents in poetry and music . . . Rhythm is, as we can see, simply the modality, the Kuntu of the Nommo. Since "man" controls things through the imperative of the word: rhythm activates the word; it is its procreative component.[8]

Jahn continues by quoting Senghor's description of rhythm as giving the word its "effective fullness" so that it is the "word of God, that is, the rhythmic word, that created the world."[9]

The indispensability of rhythm to the preached word is evident in Black preaching—whether by the consummate intellectual or the "Jackleg preacher." If the preacher is to be heard and felt by the African American congregation, there must be a rhythmic delivery of the sermon. In Black preaching, the sermon is both prose and poem. The sermon is a poetic production in narrative form, much like James Baldwin's *Go Tell It on the Mountain*, Langston Hughes's "Ballad of the Landlord," or James Weldon Johnson's *God's Trombones*.

This chapter attempts to describe something extraordinary, something that to a large degree must be witnessed and experienced in order to be captured fully and described adequately. As a participant-observer in this phenomenal enterprise, I hereby describe this reality in an effort to construct a hermeneutic of preaching style—orality, aurality, and gesturality.

Embodied Preaching: Gestures

African American preaching, unlike some of the straitjacket preaching of traditional Eurocentric homiletics, is an oral and gestural activity. This does not mean that it is not an intellectual activity, but in the tradition of African American preaching and the language of the Black church, "the activity of the limbs" contributes to the meaning of preaching by creating a dialogue with the self and the hearer. This is a critical, albeit ancillary, element of African American preaching and often helps to make the more substantive theological and hermeneutical ingredients more palatable because they become integrated into the whole preaching process.

When the preacher preaches to himself or herself and when the soul of the self responds, then the congregation also responds to the entire message and person. More precisely, the eloquence of the preacher's syncopated voice often synchronizes with the gestures of the hands, arms, legs, and face to create a dialogue with the text and the congregation. For example, some of the most beloved preachers in the African American community are very oral and gestural—using voice and body to help communicate and interpret the gospel. I think of Dr. Manuel Scott, a rather diminutive man in physical stature, but a giant of a preacher with a giant message.[10] He often speaks an eloquent word and then demonstrates its power by moving his hands and arms, scratching his head, or exemplifying some other facial expression.

The way in which the preacher shares the word contributes to the word. This helps to convey the power of the gospel. David James Randolph asserts, "Persons communicate by the way in which they speak as well as by the content of their speech."[11] The preacher does this better and more frequently than any other communicator in the African American community. Not even an orator, president, or politician as renowned as John F. Kennedy in his State of the Union address or a lawyer as popular as Johnnie Cochran in his summation to the jury, or a poet as beloved as Nikki Giovanni or Amari' Baraku is any more eloquent than the preacher.

The preacher indeed has a way of speaking that is unique, and when that is coupled with gospel content, one is able to distinguish this speech from all other forms of speech. When I think of amalgamated eloquence and content in speech—that is, the oral elegance of preaching—several of my own mentors, teachers, and colleagues come to mind. For example, Miles Jerome Jones[12] preached as Paul declares in "demonstration of the Spirit."[13] He could take a word, almost any word—even a word meaningless on the surface, like an article or a conjunction—and transform it into a meaningful theological treatise. Again, Miles Jones's ability to work with a word in the creation and development of the sermonic word attests to the fact that orality and gesturality are integral to African American preaching. Like Manuel Scott, he too would often move his limbs, especially his hands, in a way that contributed to interpreting and understanding the sermon. The synchrony that exists between gestures of the face, hands, legs, and feet vis-à-vis the orality and content of the sermon is clearly seen and heard in Black preaching. I also refer to this as "linguistic play" in my book *Preaching Liberation*: "Linguistic play is taking a word in its scriptural context, and bouncing it to and fro, cajoling it carefully and squeezing it . . . and extrapolating from that word every possible meaning."[14]

Other examples of this masterful orality and gesturality in preaching are Charles Adams (often called the "Harvard Whooper" because of his ability to balance and synchronize his education with the spiritual nature of African American preaching) and James Perkins, who speaks with a rapid cadence and keeps time with his whole body, particularly his feet, with a marching-in-place motion throughout the preaching event.

An Embodied Hermeneutic

However, I believe it is that and *something else* that draw people from miles and miles to hear these men preach. It is because they too preach in "demonstration of the Spirit." The power of the Holy Spirit cannot be restrained and contained, and quite frankly, little or no time needs to be devoted to such an enterprise except to say that traditional African American preaching is more than "animated conversation," as some scholars have described it. A book on the substance and technique of successful Christian preaching entitled *The Secret of Preaching Power* by Simon Blocker asserts that "the best formula for delivery as far as voice and tonal quality are concerned is contained in the two words 'animated conversation.'"[15] He later explains, however, that this animated conversation means that "everything must be under control,"[16] and he states, "Do not feel that you have to gesture . . . If you are so filled and thrilled by the message that you simply have to make gestures, make them graceful but not excessive."[17] While this advice to preachers is dated and directed toward whites, African American preachers are gracefully doing what I believe comes naturally—delivering sermons with their body and soul, unrestrained by the so-called proper pulpit etiquette that translates historically in mainline Protestant churches into what some refer to as boring, dry, and sleep-inducing preaching. African American preaching, in the language of young Black rapper Q-Tip, is "a vivrant thing."[18]

Henry H. Mitchell has written extensively on Black preaching and is acknowledged universally as one who has contributed enormously to our understanding of this art.[19] Mitchell, who has brought the term *celebration* in Black preaching to the forefront of homiletic discussion, says, "The Black climax, at its best, is a kind of celebration of the goodness of God and the standing of Black people in his Kingdom, as these elements have been expressed in the message."[20] In other words, it manifests itself stylistically; however, it is something more than style: *an embodied hermeneutic!*

This is akin to Friedrich Nietzsche's notion that form for the artist (i.e., the preacher) is also content, and content is often that which the nonartist calls "form." Don M. Wardlaw says, "Sermon form, then becomes a hermeneutic in itself, releasing the scriptural word among the hearers through the liberated expression of the preacher."[21] The liberated expressions of the preacher constitute substance to the African American preacher because style and substance, like the sacred and the secular, cannot be dichotomized or bifurcated. Moreover, Thomas G. Long makes a similar point when he explains the relationship between the scriptural form and the content and meaning of the text. He states:

> Texts are not packages containing ideas; they are means of communication. When we ourselves ask what a text means, we are not searching for the idea of the text. We are trying to discover its total impact upon a reader—and everything about a text works together to create that impact. We may casually speak of the *form* and the *content* of a text as if they were two separate realities, but if "content" is used as a synonym for "meaning," the form must be seen as a vital part of the content.[22]

Although there are indeed some bifurcated notions and practices at work in the African American church, preaching may not be construed as one of them. Cleophus J. LaRue adds clarity to this point when he states, "The power of black preaching is not uniquely derivative of style or technique but of how blacks perceive God as a result of their experiences and their interpretation of scripture based on those experiences."[23] African American preaching is a unique melding of experience and scripture, thereby resulting in an embodied hermeneutic that reflects particularly their encounter with God. More and more, I have come to believe that when taken seriously, none of the components of Black preaching are really ancillary, and the essence of the sermon is an amalgamation of its constituent parts—including its delivery. John Malcus Ellison, who served as catechist for my ordination, contends:

> Pulpit drama, therefore, never refers to applied art but rather to the innate qualities of sincerity, integrity of feeling and dominance of "soul energy." These natural elements of drama are reflected in the minister's personality—face, eyes, voice and gestures. Dramatic expression is saying with action what words cannot say. *Deep feelings elude words. To express them requires action and symbolism.*[24]

Again, Ellison notes that the preacher often uses his or her whole body and mind in dramatizing the sermon as an extension of exegesis and hermeneutics. This holistic manifestation of homiletical depth is indicative of the preaching we often hear, see, and witness in the African American community.

Whenever the preacher mounts the pulpit, he or she is practicing the art of interpretation. To interpret a text is to explain, to expound on, or to translate the text in a language or expression that conveys its meaning with clarity. Interpretation in preaching, then, is the translation of a text for the community of faith. Steven Mailloux points out, "Translation is always an approximation, which is to say that interpretation is always directed. It is always an approximation of something, it is always directed toward something: situations, actions, gestures."[25] Additionally, Dr. Ellison's words provide a perfect parallel to what the writer is suggesting. He says that deep feelings often elude words, so the sermon requires action and symbolism, that is, gesturality.

Finally, some expressions are too deep for words. Howard Thurman would often search for words in absolute silence, thereby filling an auditorium—chapel or church sanctuary—with awe and expectation. Thurman represents the archetype of expression that is beyond the luring captivity of words. Indeed, when the power of the Holy Spirit guides and directs the preacher, the sermon becomes an event characterized by actions and expressions too deep for words. Again, this writer and thousands of others have witnessed this in African American churches time and time again, where there was a tarrying of the Holy Spirit that was prolonged by the spontaneous eruptions of moans, shrieks, tears, shouts, and other manifestations of emotions and the Spirit by the hearers. This phenomenon is what I suspect Paul meant when he said that the Spirit speaks a language that is indeed too deep for words: "These things God has revealed to us through the Spirit; for the Spirit searches everything, even the depths of God" (1 Corinthians 2:10, NRSV).

Gesture as Symbolic Language

Gesturing is not secondary to language but is a part of language. Indeed, it is a language that is older than speech and written discourse and may have prompted Ferdinand de Saussure to write:

First, no one has proved that speech, as it manifests itself
when we speak, is entirely natural . . . For instance Whitney,
to whom language is one of several social institutions,
thinks that we use the vocal apparatus as the instrument of
language purely through luck, for the sake of convenience:
men might just as well have chosen gestures and used visual
symbols instead of acoustical symbols.[26]

Gestures in preaching seem to be ubiquitous among African
Americans. This is usually not mere histrionics but an essential
form of communication that seems to contribute to understanding the sermon in African American churches. Even
Friedrich Nietzsche emphasizes the effectiveness of this mode
of communication:

Older than language is the mimicking of gestures, which
takes place involuntarily and is even now, when the language of gesture is universally restrained and control of the
muscles has been achieved . . . The imitated gesture leads
him who imitates it back to the sensation which it expressed
in the face or body of the person imitated. That is how people learned to understand one another: that is how a child
still learns to understand its mother . . . As soon as the
meaning of gestures was understood, a *symbolism* of gestures could arise: I mean a sign language of sounds could be
so agreed that at first one produced sound *and* gesture (to
which it was symbolically joined), later only the sound.[27]

The gesture is the ultimate symbol, metaphor, and figure. It
is the failure of spoken language to capture the ultimate meaning, tone, and "feeling" of the text. It is an effort, albeit
speechless, to interpret existence with the most basic element
of existence, the body or body language. Then again, these

gestures do have their own form of language—speech that says something to the hearer who has already heard words. When the sound of words or spoken language needs to be augmented, only a demonstration will suffice. Jacques Derrida makes this clear when he says, "In French, too, the *demonstration*, with an accent, can be, first and foremost, a gesture, a movement of the body, the act of a 'manifestation.'"[28]

In African American preaching, there is evidence that the actions—that is, body movement, facial expressions, etc.—serve to project meaning in the sermon. These aesthetic elements contribute to the sermon's content. In this connection, philosopher Herbert Marcuse asserts, "Aesthetic form is not opposed to content, not even dialectically. In the work of art, form becomes content and vice versa."[29] African American preaching like preaching in general is indeed a work of art.

A Soulful Sound: The Aural and the Oral

Aurality and orality in preaching are further constituted by two other elements, namely rhythm and cadence. These are critical codeterminants of homiletic effectiveness, and any true understanding of the African American sermon must consider the nature of preaching and its impact on the hearer. Moreover, the preacher should not become disconnected from the biblical text, because when this happens, the preacher becomes more of orator, which is not the same as being a preacher!

The biblical text is the preacher's main tool for expounding on the word of God. However, the context and the experiences of the preacher and the congregation all play a critical role in understanding and interpreting the text. The text is not an old, isolated relic of the past that is irrelevant to the needs of today. It does, however, need to be interpreted and reinterpreted for the community in which it is being used. This means that the preacher must ferret out of the text its meaning for people who seek to be scriptural—forgoing the precarious prating and prattling of the comic or comedian, who often mimics the preacher as a verbose, empty talker.

Rhythm and Cadence in Preaching

I am increasingly convinced that the musical, rhythmic nature of Black preaching is a vital component of its heart and soul. The content of the sermon is vital and is a necessary corollary to its form. However, for years, I have sought to ground the import of preaching in theory, philosophy, literature, and linguistics, but I have been unable to make such a claim stick. Every time I think I have classified a sermon or identified its strengths and weaknesses structurally, methodologically, and content-wise, I find the flaws in my own analysis by realizing that something has not been captured by my content analysis. This is true because the sermon is certainly more than content and method, and its essence and affect are often embedded in style, culture, and the psyche—that which is in some sense beyond method—what I prefer to call the aesthetic dimension of preaching. Moreover, method is indeed a necessary prerequisite for sermon preparation. The sermon is very much "a happening," as W. E. B. Du Bois described it.

A perfect example is often seen in my preaching classes as well as in churches. A student or pastor will preach a sermon that fails to capture the elements of method, hermeneutic precision, theological truth, or the many other textual and architectural details of construction. Nevertheless, the class or in some cases the local congregation will be standing on their feet, cheering and hollering or weeping and wailing with joy and happiness, that is, spiritual ecstasy in response to the preached word. While this is not enough to merit an extraordinary grade or a glowing evaluation, it forces me to try to locate the core, the common denominator involved in popular preaching to the folk who constitute the local church in the Black community. Also, I have had the opportunity to preach in many places, from the chapel at Princeton to some large urban churches, to rural small congregations in the land of my mother and father (Virginia and North Carolina), and my own rhythmic cadence often determines the degree to which my sermon is received and perceived by the masses as an effective and affective communicative discourse.

This deep core connection to the masses of people is a necessary component of sermon delivery or preaching style in the African American tradition. Moreover, there are elements of story, as we will explore in the next chapter. However, in traditional African American preaching, there seems to be some other phenomenon integral to the orality of the enterprise that captures the heart and soul of the hearer. I don't think that this can be easily captured, identified, classified, or categorized, but I believe that the correlation between that which is spoken and that which is heard and felt is partially determined by the rhythm and cadence of the preacher's voice—the ebb and flow of the words that emanate from the heart and soul of the preacher. In the mind of the hearer, the orality of the sermon and the eloquence of the preacher's speech are often "sweet" to hear and sometimes outweigh and possibly obviate flaws in the content of the sermon, creating a new hermeneutic grounded in the "style" of the preacher. As an African American preacher and teacher, I have often had this experience. The sermon is like music to the hearer's ears, and the congregation responds by affirming the power of the gospel via the spoken word. Something happens in the hearing of the sermon that makes the hearer want to shout or cry, and often this has as much to do with sound as with substance or is certainly a merger of the two.

Like rhythm, cadence in preaching is critical to the receptivity of the hearer. Cadence is like the stride and stroke of sound flowing from the preacher's mouth with power that pricks the spiritual and emotional strands of consciousness within the hearer's heart and soul. Some of the well-known preachers in the Black community have a cadence, a stride that envelops the church within its nectar-like grasp, and like that staple of early-childhood stories and folklore, "Tar Baby," it grabs and holds your attention—refusing to let go of your heart, your desire to be blessed by the power of the spoken word of God. There is something about this stride toward ecstatic freedom, this galloping sound of words and phrases about the God of our salvation that engulfs and captures and helps one cope with the "troubles of this world."

Cadence is a critical component of the preaching process, and when coupled with rhythm, it becomes an awesome combination in the quest for a cultural homiletical hermeneutic. This is not the same as content; however, the merging of content and form is a prerequisite for good, effective preaching. It is important to realize that one without the other makes for dull preaching. As I said earlier, form and substance are interconnected to the extent that one without the other makes for something less than a powerful sermon. African American preaching has uniquely combined these two elements such that a natural nexus now unites them. Nevertheless, form or "style" is a constitutive element of content in African American preaching, and the preacher who has mastered both has a much better chance of surviving and excelling in the African American church than the preacher who has mastered one at the expense of the other, thereby bifurcating style and substance as if they are two separate entities.

Usually, a more musical style or a more syncopated tone and cadence constitutes "preaching" in the Black church tradition. This modulated inflection of the voice typified by persons such as Martin Luther King Jr. or the myriad Black preachers throughout the land is understood by the masses as the critical element in preaching. Although style and content are inextricably linked, style seems to be more overwhelming and more satiating to the hearer than content. However, this does not obviate the importance of nor the necessity for a strong coherent (substantive) component that will augment and facilitate the glaring nature of style.

Style Switching

In Black preaching, there are hearers who wait until a certain transition in the sermon occurs before they get involved. This often means that the hearers think "real" preaching has taken place when there is a shift in cadence and tonality. This shift usually takes place somewhere near the end of the sermon, after the preacher has made the more difficult conceptual points. As a matter of fact, some people have told me that they are very uninterested in the first part of the sermon and only begin to pay attention when the *tone* changes. With many preachers, the shift is very gradual, yet the sermon becomes markedly different from what occurred prior to this transition in tone and cadence.

Thus, it is commonplace for the preacher in the African American tradition to practice a double style of delivering the word. This is characterized by a slow to moderate speech pattern at the beginning of the sermon that gradually picks up as the sermon develops. The preacher can be said to switch from a more didactic, formal style to a more kerygmatic and improvisational or "jazzlike" style. This is akin to what the philosopher Theophus H. Smith calls "style switching" in his discussion of communication through music. A recent trend led by popular culture–oriented televangelists is a cous on what they call "teaching," which has a style of its own. This method is a "switch" to a different paradigm of performance. Television by its nature demands a new set of props and an entertaining presentation.

The following sermon applies elements from the aesthetic dimension of preaching to a message about the story of Jonah. As you read, consider how gestures and vocal tones can bring these words to life, and try to identify where "style switching" occurs. Also consider your own experiences as a hearer of sermons. What style of preaching engages your intellect and your emotions? When has a preacher inspired you to act?

Sermon *Second Chances*

> The word of the LORD came to Jonah a second time, saying, "Get up, go to Nineveh, that great city, and proclaim to it the message that I tell you." So Jonah set out and went to Nineveh, according to the word of the LORD.
>
> —Jonah 3:1–3a, NRSV

Many of us today have wasted and squandered money and opportunities. We have faltered and failed in so many ways to do what God has called us to do, yet we have had so little compassion for others. It seems that we are so quick to condemn the faults and failures of others, oftentimes so eager to accuse, point a finger, and judge someone else for their human weaknesses, and their failures, their slips of conscience and their acquiescence to the luring power of the flesh—the body. We have a condemning air about us, an arrogant spirit of superiority that suggests that we have never done anything wrong—that we have never lied, that we have never fornicated nor committed adultery, that we have never deceived or tricked or schemed, that we have never been homeless or poor or hungry. We act as if we are perfect and everybody else is in need of salvation—everybody except us.

Jonah teaches us that we are not perfect, that failure is a part of the human condition, that life includes failure, and if we are going to be saved, we have to learn to cope with the ups and downs of life. Jonah has disobeyed God, he has ignored the call of God, he has gone in the wrong direction, he has been thrown overboard, he has been swallowed up by a whale, he has prayed to the Lord from the belly of the whale. Jonah has been to hell and back. He has been in the deep, dark dungeons of Sheol—but God was still there. You can run, but you cannot get away from God.

But while folk in the church—folk in the pews and in the choir stands, folk in church school, deacons and trustees—may be slow to forgive and quick to judge their fellow brothers and sisters, God is a God of *second chances*. God does not write us off even if we go in the wrong directions, God does not abandon us even if we go down the wrong path, on the wrong boat, causing chaos and stormy weather for others. Yes, Jonah was disobedient; yes, Jonah was hardheaded; yes, Jonah was obstinate and ugly in his behavior and attitude; yes, Jonah was determined to do what he wanted to do, so much like so many folk in the church determined to disobey God, determined to disregard the word of the Lord. But the sweetest, most gracious words of scripture are found in this text. The most loving and kindest words of prophetic literature are found in this text. The words of this text contain words that describe the essential nature of God as a God who gives us second chances.

Don't write people off, don't be unforgiving, don't be mad and unkind, and don't be rigid and inflexible in your relationship with others. Give folk a second chance! God is a God of second chances. God is the God who gives us the opportunity to develop a new consciousness, a second time. Let's look at the text more closely to learn a few lessons from it this morning.

The first thing we glean from the text is that the message of the Lord is the same, the second time around. Second chances don't mean that the message has changed. The message is the same. The text says, "The word of the LORD came to Jonah a *second time*, saying, 'Get up, go to Nineveh, that great city.'"

Jonah still has to get up and go to Nineveh; the assignment has not changed. The destination has not changed; the mission and the mandate are still the same: go to Nineveh, that great city. The destination is the same; the place that we ran from the first time and got into a whole lot of trouble is still the place that God wants us to go. Just because Jonah had taken a holiday, an excursion on the Mediterranean Sea and caused a lot of havoc in his life and the life of the sailors, doesn't mean that his orders had changed. Just because he had gone AWOL did not mean that God had changed his orders. And although Jonah had said *no!* the first time, when God came to him the second time, God said the same thing: Go to Nineveh!

God's orders are the same, Second Baptist! Go to Nineveh! Do what I ask you to do. Go to the jails and prisons, go to the schools and street corners, go to those who are hopeless, go to Nineveh, that great city, where the power brokers reside, go to Nineveh. Go where I send you. Second chances give us an opportunity to do what we didn't do the first time.

Second, not only are you to go to Nineveh, but you go to do the same thing I told you the first time. Going is not enough, but the purpose for your going is to preach! Proclaim the message that I tell you! The text says, "The word of the Lord came to Jonah a second time, saying, 'Arise, get up, go to Nineveh, that great city, and proclaim, preach to it the message that I tell you.'" God wanted Jonah to preach, not to philosophize or rationalize, but to preach! Not to sing or to testify, but to preach! Not to counsel or give advice to, but to preach! Not to entertain or caress folk in their carnality, in their baneful and base behavior, but to preach. Not to come in timidity and in fear, but to preach—boldly proclaiming the word of God. Jonah wasn't sent to do anything but preach, and to preach or proclaim the message that the Lord told him to preach. Not only was Jonah to preach, but the Lord said he would tell him the message. When God sends you, he will prepare you, not necessarily by divine revelation but by serious preparation, by searching and studying, by reason and experience.

It might be that Jonah is ready now to declare God's message of salvation. Jonah is ready now the second time around, to preach the message of forgiveness. After being in the belly of the whale, Jonah has a new consciousness, a new understanding of the love and grace of God. Jonah now understands God's omnipotence and his omnipresence—that God is the God of land and sea. He can now proclaim, he can preach to the people in the great city of Nineveh that God is love, that God is a prayer-hearing God, that God can rescue you from the clutches of death and give you a second chance. And this time you can preach what the Lord tells you to preach, not what you want to say, not what folk want to hear, not what tickles the fancy and satisfies the power brokers in the church and community, but you can preach what God tells you to proclaim—what you have endured, what you have witnessed, what you have experienced, what you know in your soul.

Go to Nineveh, go to the great city and preach, proclaim not what the powerful are saying, nor what you learned about German philosophy or Reformed theology—not Immanuel Kant or Hegel or Martin Luther or John Calvin, but preach what I tell you. I don't have a message of my own. I don't have anything to say to the church on my own. I'm too weak, I am too selfish, I am too afraid, I am too rebellious, I am too ignorant, I am too much of a failure like Jonah to have a message of my own; I must proclaim the message that God tells me to preach!

Finally, second chances enable us to turn our "no" into a "yes." In chapter 1, when "the word of the LORD came to Jonah son of Amittai, saying, 'Go at once to Nineveh, that great city, and cry out against it; for their wickedness has come up before me'" (NRSV), Jonah said no and went to Tarshish, fleeing from the presence of the Lord. But now after all he has been through, now Jonah has a second chance, and he says, "Yes, Lord, I'll go where you tell me to go! Yes, Lord, I'll say what you tell me to say, because when I did what I wanted to do, I failed. When I did what I wanted to do, I almost died. When I did what I wanted to do, I almost had a whole ship of sailors destroyed. When I did what I wanted to do, I lost my way. When I did what I wanted to do, I ended up in the belly of a whale. When I did what I wanted to do, I found myself at the gates of hell. When I did what I wanted to do, I was sinking deep in sin, far from the peaceful shore—now, Lord, I have a second chance, and I'm gonna use it to preach, to proclaim what you tell me to say."

God is a God of second chances. Folk have made foolish mistakes, but God uses them again; God gives them a second chance. Look at Abraham. He was willing to pass off his own wife as his sister. Again, Abraham and Sarah had given up on having a son, but God came to Abraham a second time. Come here, David: that great prophet, yet his unthinkable sin began with Bathsheba and ended with Uriah. Come, Simon Peter, who in a moment of cowardly human weakness said, "Woman, I know him not" (Luke 22:57, KJV). Jesus had said, "Peter, I know thou art going to deny me, but I have prayed for you, that you faith fail not, and when thou art converted, strengthen thy brothers." Yet on the day of Pentecost, God came to Peter a second time, and on that day he loudly proclaimed, "This is what was spoken through the prophet Joel" (Acts 2:16, NRSV). Three thousand folk were converted. Come here, Paul, ranting and raving against the church, standing in the crowd while Stephen was being stoned to death, yet on the road to Damascus, God came to him a second time.

If God could use folk like that—folk like Abraham, folk like David, folk like Peter and Paul—I know he can use us. He's a second-chance God.

5

The Sermon as Story

The distinction between telling the story and preaching is interpretation.
—Miles Jerome Jones

It is urgent that my meaning be crystal clear. The masses of men live with their backs constantly against the wall. They are the poor, the disinherited, the dispossessed.
—Howard Thurman

The act of preaching, like the sermon itself, is a work of art. The sermon is a creation, much like a musical score, a poem, or a novel. It is simultaneously a written text, a discourse, and the spoken word. The sermon is a nexus, a synchronizing of form and content. It is like a painting or a print that reflects the artist's individuality and understanding of faith and experience. It is grounded in scripture and in life, in love and pain, in the quest to be free. A sermon is an expression of life's longing to be united with God while grasping at self-understanding and authentic being. The sermon indeed is a work of art, an expression of the personality of the preacher making an axis through culture and belief in God and Jesus Christ. The sermon is a combination of imagination and hope, love and justice, power and powerlessness.

The sermon is more than exegesis, translations, word studies, and academic research on a text or topic. It cannot be divorced from the being and experiences of the preacher nor the imagination and dreams of the preacher. To be a sermon, it cannot be an essay or poem apart from the complex life experiences of the preacher. Fred Craddock makes this clear when he argues that form and content are one:

> Wherever this assumption [that content and form of expression are separate considerations] exists, almost invariably, content is on the inside and style on the outside; content is essential and form is accessory, optional. It is supposed that *matter* and *manner* are separate entities, as though one has a message which then, incidentally, is expressed in a poem or an historical event which then just happens to be cast into a story. Not so. How a speaker or singer or artist does is no subordinate dimension of what they do. How they do is what they do, and what they do is how they do it.[1]

The sermon is an act of authenticity expressed through written and spoken discourse. It is an aesthetic expression of one's being through persuasive demonstration of the Spirit. This means that the sermon must be preached with conviction and with every fiber of the mind and body if the sermon is not to be mistaken for a lecture, mimic, mime, or dramatic reading.

In this chapter I discuss several distinctive elements of African American preaching as storytelling. I am deliberately calling this "story" and not narrative because narrative preaching as a genre has been extensively explored by many scholars, among them Eugene L. Lowry and Fred Craddock. I am much indebted to them as the latter part of this chapter indicates, but some areas of African American preaching as story remain unique and have not been heretofore explored in writing, although they are practiced extensively. In particular, Black preachers invoke imagination, create sermons that use basic elements of narrative structure, and express the wisdom of African American culture in their stories and in their sermons.

African American Preaching as Imagination

When I was growing up, it was not unusual to hear and use language such as "He told a story on me," and if something were not true, one would be admonished to stop "telling stories." *Story* had at least a double meaning. On the one hand, it meant lie, but we were afraid to say that word because it was bad. Story also meant a fable, a literary creation, a tale such as "Little Red Riding Hood" or "Tar Baby." Also, the use of the word *lie* or *lying* somehow could not be used by children because it implied that one was acting too grown-up.

All stories certainly were not blatant lies, yet they all contained an element of creative fiction. My mother and father used to tell ghost stories with such vividness that I could feel the presence of a ghost as I shivered with fear. A story in the way we used it growing up in rural central Virginia was not necessarily a total and complete fabrication because some element of truth and fact often was embedded in the story, even though it would often take a cultural exegete to extrapolate the facts from the fiction. Ethical and moral truths are embedded ineluctably in fictional stories, and their fictive nature does not diminish their ethical and moral value. These values supersede the historicity of the particular story in which they are embedded. Storytelling, like preaching, is often hyperbolic in form and substance. This is very similar to what Robert Alter calls "historicized fiction"[2] and to Hans Frei's remarks that "there are highly stylized rather than realistic features in the description of Jesus and in the sequence chain in the Fourth Gospel."[3]

Imagination in Service of Love

The utilitarian and altruistic idea of the preacher as storyteller or the sermon as story is borne out in practical life. This means that if the preacher determines that the greater good or the best option for advancing the cause of love, peace, and justice or some other virtue is served by a fictive approach and response to an issue, then that response becomes the means by which love itself is advanced. Accordingly, Miles Jones defines preaching as "the action that creates the avenue for love's entrance into human affairs."[4] Preaching, then, is an act of love constituted by the necessity to help ease the pain of the suffering, the oppressed, and all those who need to hear a word of hope.

In Ernest Gaines's novel *A Lesson before Dying*, there is an ongoing dialogue between Grant, the teacher and educator, and the Reverend Ambrose, the pastor who counsels and consoles Jefferson's family while Jefferson is on death row for killing a white man, Alcee Grope, during a robbery for a pint of whiskey. Jefferson actually was not involved in the killing, but he was convicted of murder by a jury of none of his peers and sentenced to death by electrocution. This act of injustice and blatant violation of human dignity and selfhood is something the preacher faces daily.

Accordingly, the preacher in the novel, the Reverend Ambrose, develops a very practical theological perspective that is grounded in reality. His theology has the goal of alleviating suffering and pain for his people. The narrative quality in the language of the preacher is in fact no different from much of what we read in the Hebrew Bible. Robert Alter makes a poignant point when he asserts that much of biblical narrative is "historicized fiction" and epic comedy or "comic fantasy."[5] Prose fiction then has an inherent arbitrary inventiveness such that the writer mixes truth and fantasy, history and imagination to foster a quotidian understanding of reality as well as a proleptic or anticipatory hope in the hearts and minds of the people. This is exactly what the Reverend Ambrose does in Gaines's novel. In this sense, he is very much in synchrony with many of the stories in the Bible. Robert Alter makes this plain:

Under scrutiny, biblical narrative generally proves to be either fiction laying claim to a place in the chain of causation and the realm of moral consequentiality that belong to history, as in the primeval history, the tales of the patriarchs and much of the Exodus story, and the account of the early conquest, or history given the imaginative definition of fiction, as in most of the narratives from the period of the judges onward. This schema, of course, is necessarily neater than the persistently untidy reality of the variegated biblical narratives. What the Bible offers us is an uneven continuum and a constant interweaving of factual historical detail (especially, but by no means exclusively, for the later periods) with purely legendary "history"; occasional enigmatic vestiges of mythological lore; etiological stories; archetypal fictions of the founding fathers of the nation; folktales of heroes and wonder-working men of God; verisimilar inventions of wholly fictional personages attached to the progress of national history; and fictionalized versions of known historical figures. All of these narratives are presented as history, that is, as things that really happened and that have some significant consequence for human or Israelite destiny.[6]

The Reverend Ambrose, in *A Lesson before Dying*, is much more forthright and honest than some of the biblical writers in his struggle to get Grant to take the leap of faith and lie to Jefferson about his belief in the existence of heaven. The dialogue starts with the preacher talking to Grant:

> "And suppose he asks you if you believe in heaven? Then what?"
> "I hope he doesn't."
> "Suppose he do? You couldn't say yes?"
> "No, Reverend, I couldn't say yes. I couldn't lie, no matter what."
> "Not for her sake?"
> "No sir."
> The minister nodded his bald head and grunted to himself. His dark-brown eyes in that tired, weary face continued to stare back

at me. "You think you educated but you not. You think you the
only person ever had to lie? You think I never had to lie?"

"I don't know, Reverend."[7]

At this point the Reverend Ambrose begins his ethical expla-
nation of why it is necessary for him to lie. He feels that it is
his responsibility because he is serving the greater good. He
states:

> Yes, you know. You know all right. That's why you look
> down on me, because you know I lie. At wakes, at funerals,
> at weddings—Yes, I lie. I lie at wakes and funerals to relieve
> pain. 'Cause reading, writing and 'rithmetic is not enough.
> You think that's all they sent you to school for? They sent
> you to school to relieve pain, to relieve hurt—and if you
> have to lie to do it, then you lie. You lie and you lie and you
> lie. When you tell yourself you feeling good when you sick,
> you lying. When you tell other people you feeling well when
> you feeling sick, you lying. You tell them that 'cause they
> have pain too, and you don't want to add yours—and you lie.
> She been lying every day of her life, your aunt in there.
> That's how you got through that university—cheating herself
> here, cheating herself there, but always telling you she's all
> right. I've seen her hands bleed from picking cotton. I've
> seen the blisters from the hoe and the cane knife. At that
> church, crying on her knees. You ever looked at the scabs on
> her knees, boy? Course you never. Cause she never wanted
> you to see it. And that's the difference between me and you
> boy; that make me the educated one, and you the gump. I
> know my people. I know what they gone through. I know
> they done cheated themselves, lied to themselves—hoping
> that one they all love and trust can come back and help
> relieve the pain.[8]

This necessity to relieve pain and hurt is uppermost in the Reverend Ambrose's mind. He perceives this to be his ultimate

responsibility to the people he serves, and if schooling or education does not relieve pain and hurt, it falls short of its purpose.

This theory of hope and practice of situation ethics vis-à-vis the simplistic blatancy of the preacher's confession of the cor-relative dialectic between truth and lie is an effort to practice love. The preacher feels that this lie soothes the pain of the oppressed and all involved. Because he knows "what they gone through," he says, "I know my people." This epistemic under-standing of the people cannot be denied and seems to qualify the preacher's use of storytelling in a way that appears both justified and compassionate. Moreover, the preacher suggests that everybody lies and everybody is complicit one way or another—either as a silent beneficiary of another's pain or as a participant in soothing the pain of another. Moreover, because the preacher is a witness to the pain of others and Grant is not to the same degree, the preacher concludes that it is he who is the educated one, and Grant, who has been shielded from the pain and suffering of Miss Emma and Tante Lou, is in fact the gump. What is education and who is educated if the teacher or the preacher doesn't know his people? The preacher, Reverend Ambrose, interprets his context and responds accordingly. He creates a narrative, a story that brings solace to his suffering people, and like the writers of the Hebrew Bible, the preacher is a storyteller trying to build a believing community in the midst of pain and suffering.

Sanctified Imagination

The Black preacher has historically been adept in fostering and creating a new, more livable world in the minds of his or her hearers by appealing to the imagination as an interpretative tool for explicating the scriptural text and the context of oppression and injustice. In the midst of the sermon, it is not unusual even today for the preacher to seek permission from

the congregation to explore worlds beyond the text by inton-
ing, "Please let me use my sanctified imagination right here."
This becomes an interpretation tool that seeks to get around
the hegemonic nature of the historical-critical method and the
complicity of Enlightenment philosophy by imagining a world
beyond the limitations of traditional exegesis—a world imagined and embedded in hopes and dreams that cannot be sup-
pressed by either the biblical text or the social and political
context of the preacher. This is the preacher's escape hatch, a
secret weapon to not be captive and confined by the western
canon or the explicitness of the written biblical text. Imagination has no rules and no restraints such as the written text may
imply or suggest. Imagination is freedom to explore and to
dream a new meaning, a new world, a new understanding of a
given text.

The voice of the text is not limited to or restrained by the
intent of the author. This flies in the face of the historical-
critical method. But it is more reflective of the midrashic way
of interpretation, as Walter Brueggemann suggests.[9] The act of
imagination is grounded in the text itself, and this makes
imagination in preaching both a textual and extratextual
enterprise. It is beyond the text in the sense that it is a subversive act of interpretation that depends not on the exegesis or
interpretation of well-known scholars, but on the needs of the
people in a particular context. Brueggemann says, "Texts are
open to many meanings, more than one of which may be legitimate and faithful at the same time."[10]

The sanctified imagination of Black preachers is akin to the
discourse of novels and poetry, where the writer imagines
another world and takes the reader there. Similarly, the
preacher has the responsibility to help people who are burdened by forces of denial and hatred both internally and exter-
nally to think or imagine something else—a world where
justice, fairness, peace, love, and righteousness prevail. "The

preacher traffics in a 'fiction' that he or she makes true. But that is why preaching is so urgent and must be done with such artistic zeal and integrity. This world of the gospel is not 'real,' not available until this credible utterance authorizes a departure from a failed text and appropriation of this text."[11] African Americans have been able to imagine a world where justice, fairness, and love prevail. This imagined world allows one to cope with the evils and injustices in the world. The imagined world has been a place where "all of God's children have shoes" and there is an end to the "troubles of this world."

Slavery is based on a lie, and that lie is that the white man is superior to the black man. Moreover, everybody involved in the culture participates in the lie. Brian K. Blount quotes Lewis Clarke in reference to liberation:

> Of course, the slaves don't tell folks what's passing in their minds about freedom; for they know what'll come of it if they do . . . The fact is, slavery's the father of lies. The slave knows he ought to have his freedom; and his master knows it, just as well as he does; but they both say they don't; and they tell me some folks this way believe 'em. The master say the slave don't want his freedom, and the slave says he don't want it; but they both of 'em lies, and know it.[12]

Lying is a way of doing what Blount calls "reconfiguring reality," and slaves used the Bible as their chief accomplice in this reconfiguration process. Moreover, because the white slave master and his progenitors are the architects of the lie, the slaves learned from him how to preserve their lives and to foster a liberation hermeneutic based on their own efforts to survive. Their lying was grounded in the quest for freedom and liberation for the entire group as a people, as a community— not for personal gain or greed. Brian Blount states:

And so the slaves maintained what was in effect a "code of silence" to protect others who had committed acts the owners or overseer considered unethical. Hiding the shelters of runaways or the identities of those who had stolen the master's property or the locations of the "hush harbors" where clandestine acts of independent worship took place or the identities of those who prayed and worshipped for freedom or the hostile and hateful feelings toward the master and mistress was expected, even if lying and subterfuge were necessary to do it.[13]

Blount goes on to argue that the slaves reconfigured ethics, including masking their true feelings, outright lying and deceit, theft, and some other acts of defiance.[14]

Inherent in the lying was the spirit of truth and freedom vis-à-vis the quest for liberation—not personal gain, but freedom for the entire oppressed community.

Imagination in the mind of the slave was critical to the creation of a new existence, as well as a survival strategy. This imagination allowed the slave to reconstitute morality and to redefine virtue and ultimately provided a new understanding of untruth. This means that untruth became more important than truth in advancing the cause of justice and freedom for the entire community.

Being and the Imagination

The sermon as a work of art, like the poem or the piece of music, is grounded in imagination. R. G. Coolingwood says, "The work of art proper is something not seen or heard, but something imagined. But what is it that we imagine?"[15] The sermon creates a world where "all God's children got shoes" or where "everybody talking about heaven ain't going there." The imagination of the Black preacher has helped to foster a culture and create a world.

Gordon Kaufman, in his book *The Theological Imagination*, says:

> I have become persuaded that theology is (and always has been) essentially a constructive work of the human imagination, an expression of the imagination's activity helping to provide orientation for human life through developing a symbolical "picture" of the world roundabout and of the human place within that world. In the course of history the fertile human imagination has generated, in the great religious and cultural traditions of humankind, a number of very diverse views of the world and of the human.[16]

Likewise, James Engell connects self-understanding and self-consciousness to a tradition of philosophical inquiry:

> The ideal lives in and through the actual. Imagination creates the real image, the living language and symbol of ideal reason. Imagination potentizes reason, releases its potential, and makes ideas productive: they appear in material form. Only imagination, then, can direct us to the highest calling of philosophy—the absolute, or God. And since art is the activity of man, which most closely resembles the creative imagination of God, the highest philosophy is the philosophy of art.[17]

Preaching is indeed a sacred art. The construction of the sermon and its delivery are an artistic enterprise that employs the imagination. James Weldon Johnson, in his classic *God's Trombones*, refers to the old-time Black preacher in language that is certainly sexist by today's standards:

> He preached a personal and anthropomorphic God, a sure-enough heaven and a red-hot hell. His imagination was bold and unfettered. He had the power to sweep his hearers before him; and so himself was often swept away.[18]

In praying for the preacher to be sanctified and able to preach with power and imagination, Johnson's prayer, "Listen Lord," captures this spirit:

> And now, O Lord, this man of God,
> Who breaks the bread of life this morning—
> Shadow him in the hollow of thy hand,
> And keep him out of the gunshot of the devil.
> Take him, Lord—this morning—
> Wash him with hyssop inside and out,
> Hang him up and drain him dry of sin.
> Pin his ear to the wisdom-post,
> And make his words sledgehammers of truth—
> Beating on the iron heart of sin.
> Lord God, this morning—
> Put his eye to the telescope of eternity,
> And let him look upon the paper walls of time.
> Lord, turpentine his imagination,
> Put perpetual motion in his arms,
> Fill him full of the dynamite of thy power,
> Anoint him all over with the oil of thy salvation,
> And set his tongue on fire.[19]

Telling the Story: Narrative Structure in Sermons

Sunday after Sunday, in pulpits across the United States and the world, sermons and stories are constructed and heralded as a word from the Lord. For those committed to the homiletical enterprise, the search for new methods of effective preaching never ends. For a wealth of ideas, we should consider the traditions of African American preachers, who practiced a well-crafted form of narrative preaching long before its terminology and nomenclature became a part of the homiletical lexicon.

What is narrative preaching? According to Eugene Lowry, the narrative sermon involves a story told with a major plot that begins with a discrepancy or conflict, "makes its way through complication" (pointing out that things always get worse), makes a decisive reversal of fate, and "then moves finally toward resolution or closure."[20] Lowry points out that the preacher may feel called upon to use a narrative (or tell a story) within the narrative sermon. The sermon is marked by temporal sequencing, which may refer to source (narrative biblical text) or presentation (narrative discourse).[21] Wayne Robinson defines the narrative sermon as "an event-in-time that moves from opening disequilibrium (or conflict) through escalation (complication) to surprising reversal (peretia) into closing denouement."[22] Jeffrey Arthurs states that a "first-person narrative sermon" involves expounding and applying a biblical text by retelling the story through the perspective of a character in the story.[23] The personality of the preacher is subordinated to the personality of a narrator, who is an observer of or participant in the story. From these various definitions of narrative preaching, we can conclude that narrative preaching begins with conflict, makes its path through complications, and presses toward a resolution to the conflict that will enable the listeners to live better and become better persons.[24]

In addition to these attributes, narrative sermons are characterized by a narrative sequence and strategic delay. The narrative sequence, according to Eugene Lowry, is the unfolding of the bind or plot in the story by some discrepancy or loss of equilibrium, an attempt at resolution, and then the consequences for good and evil actions.[25] Strategic delay is the deliberate refusal to announce in advance a conclusion, moral, or resolution of the problem in the story or biblical text. It is a good way to clarify and explain every dimension of the story that burdens the plot and encumbers progress toward solution.

It is a way to avoid letting the cat out of the bag. This can be done through the vehicle of many literary forms. Fred Craddock describes the method of narrative preaching this way:

> By narrative structure I am not proposing . . . a long story or a series of stories or illustrations. While such may actually be the form used for a given message, it is not necessary in order to be narrative. Communication may be narrativelike and yet contain a rich variety of material: poetry, polemic, anecdote, humor, exegetical analysis, commentary.[26]

When the word *narrative* is used within the discipline of homiletics, it is important to carefully discern the manner in which the word is applied to the actual process of preaching. A hermeneutical approach to narrative preaching can involve the form or content of the sermon—or both. For many preachers, it is the narrative or literary form of the biblical text which should guide the preacher in developing the sermon. But other ways are used to incorporate aspects of narrative into the preacher's use of biblical materials. For example, Richard Thulin invites the homiletician to retell biblical narratives, Henry Mitchell and James Sanders implore the preacher to identify creatively with characters in biblical narratives, and Charles Rice asks the preacher to discover the manner in which the contemporary human story can be imaginatively discovered in the metaphors and images of the biblical story. Regardless of the biblically oriented approach to narrative preaching used, confusion is possible and likely unless sharply refined clarification is made.

Critiques of Narrative Preaching

One challenge to narrative preaching is that many critics say that it is pseudo-homiletical and is not really preaching.

Narrative preaching was originally hailed as the strategy (found by Fred Craddock) that would save pulpits from damaging irrelevancy. It now faces pointed criticism at the hands of people who see it as the hallmark of the troubled church and world. William H. Willimon laments the fact that many preachers have jettisoned solid exposition and rational argument in favor of storytelling and pulpit drama. This way of doing homiletics, Willimon argues, represents a dangerous capitulation to a culture shaped by modern media. For in an attempt to make the gospel palatable to contemporary listeners, preachers have replaced sermons that explain with those that entertain. These sermons, Willimon contends, are often no more than

> a string of disconnected images without transition, each image with a different degree of emotional intensity because, like TV producers, we do not want our hearers to make connections, to set thoughts in context, to raise questions of overall coherence. Nor does our congregation desire such coherence; TV has created an audience that expects to receive its information in a detached, episodic way, with emotional response, but without thought.[27]

While Willimon's description of narrative preaching is a bit exaggerated and on the verge of caricature, his theological criticisms are very sound. When narrative sermons are nothing more than culturally appealing—though theologically empty— episodes of pulpit entertainment, then they lead to spiritual malnutrition. Although such preaching has the potential to be didactically fulfilling, it feeds homiletical mush to churches that hunger for the food of substance: "There is no lack of information in a Christian Land; something else is lacking; and this is a something which the one man cannot directly communicate to the other."[28]

Similarly, Hans Frei presents a valid concern, which centers on the issue of the separation of biblical content and form. As Frei puts it, the scripture "simultaneously . . . depicts and renders the reality . . . of what it talks about."[29] So the split happened, the "great reversal" in which, unfortunately, the biblical story was made to fit "into another world with another story rather than incorporating that world into the biblical story."[30] The texts are seemingly emptied of their own reality and treated only as symbolic expressions of an allegedly deeper truth.

In the early 1960s, homileticians assembled themselves in an attempt to revitalize the practice of effective preaching. In the late 1960s, Fred Craddock recommended a slate of significant reforms that would honor the Christological tradition of preaching and at the same time honor the authenticity and flow of the biblical record. Among his recommended change for homiletics, Craddock introduced a new approach for designing sermons—the inductive method—that promised to value the role of the listener in the preaching event. This event proved to be pivotal because Craddock directed our attention toward the way in which people listen and process story. This proved to be the origin of narrative preaching in the form that we now know it.

Creating a Narrative Sermon

The methodology of a well-written narrative sermon can help the preacher forge a strong union of homiletics and storytelling. What are the necessary steps to using narrative structure in a sermon? What narrative components should be included? Eugene Lowry suggests the following method for constructing a narrative sermon.[31]

Two preliminary stages typically occur and should occur before the stage of sermonic formation. The first stage involves prayerful thoughts that involve (1) jotting down some notes about possible sermon ideas, (2) reading the daily lectionary passages, (3) consulting a file of notes and sermon ideas, and (4) checking with the denominational calendar when applicable. The second preliminary stage is the stage of decision, when the preacher settles on the idea that is to be shaped into narrative homiletical form. This stage represents a transition to a very peculiar state of knowing implicitly that a sermon can and will happen, but not knowing precisely what the sermon will be. This is when we can say, "We have a word."

When preparing for and preaching a sermon, remember that you have to tell the congregation what you're going to tell them, tell them what you have to tell them, and then tell them what you told them. This sets the stage for a dramatic tension introduced within the sermon. This tension is the plot—which is key to both the preparation and presentation of the sermon.

In the construction of narrative sermons, two plot forms are available. The first kind is the "typical movie plot," which begins with a felt discrepancy and moves to an unknown solution. This kind of plot hinges upon a particular dilemma and usually a painful choice that has to be made by the main character(s) or protagonist in the story. Those outside of the story (the congregation) are caught by this basic discrepancy (the protagonist's bind); their attention is fastened on the ambiguity of the suspense. The story's plot or the sermon continues to thicken until it moves finally to a resolution unknown to anyone in advance.

The second kind of plot is called the "television series plot," which begins with a felt discrepancy (just like the aforementioned movie plot) but moves toward a known conclusion (unlike the movie plot). In this second kind of plot, the audience knows that the protagonist will survive, make it through, and everything will be all right, but that's not the question. The real question within this particular plot is, "how?"

Usually, the sermon is more effective if it uses the television series plot. The congregation has gathered to worship God.

Symbols of all kinds have already made the central affirmation of the goodness of God before the sermon begins. The congregation is sitting with eager expectation, waiting for the gospel to be proclaimed one way or another, and for Jesus Christ to emerge as Savior and Lord (which is oftentimes the answer to the sermonic bind). But how? In what way? For what purpose? This unknown middle ground provides the context for effective sermonic tension.

The plot within the narrative sermon must catch people in the very depths of the awful discrepancies and dilemmas of their world, social and personal. It is to these very real discrepancies that the gospel of Jesus Christ is addressed. Sometimes it appears that perhaps there is absolutely no redemptive answer to the human predicament. This is the bind people feel as ambiguity, and this dilemma is the central question in every sermon. How can the gospel intersect with the particulars of the human experience and come out on the other side in resolution? This question *is* the forming of the sermonic plot.

Because the narrative sermon is seen as an event in time, existing in time, not space (a process versus a collection of parts constructing a whole), it is helpful to think of the flow of a narrative sermon as sequence rather than structure.

Reinhold Niebuhr speaks of the anxiety consequence of our being both finite and self-transcendent, and some psychologists call humans "homeless animals," "freaks of the universe."[32] Ambiguity that is established in this first stage is looked upon as a foe that needs to be vanquished. The need to resolve ambiguity is theological in nature and can be used effectively in writing sermons. It heightens the listeners' attention and places them on the edge of their seats in expectation. One cannot rest easy until some solution occurs, and the result is both a knowing and a feeling.

This first stage of a narrative sermon is designed to stimulate interest. This is caused by presenting ambiguity that is directly related to the central theme of the sermon. There is always one major discrepancy, bind, or problem that is the main issue and seeks to be resolved. The central task of any sermon, therefore, is the resolution of that particular central ambiguity. There can and may be other minor ambiguities along the progression of the sermon, but the preacher must be deliberate in keeping the central ambiguity—the main problem—in focus. This allows the listener to anticipate a better future by the resolution of the central issue or problem.[33]

Cultural Origins of Storytelling

Effective sermons, like good stories, are rooted in culture. Storytelling and narration come directly from culture. Storytelling is as old as humanity itself. At the very beginning of human history, we find storytelling (mainly in the tribal sense). In Ur of the Sumerians over ten thousand years ago, we first encounter the oral epic. The ancient Minoans had their cycles of stories. Homer in Asia Minor was one of the greatest storytellers of all times. The Hebrew people had a unique genius for storytelling (as indicated in the Old Testament), and rich stories perdure from country to country, tribe to tribe, person to person all over the continent of Africa. People by nature are storytellers, and this fact provides a strong backbone and foundation for culture.

Whatever the form, stories and narrative are ways in which a community and individuals in a community express who they are and what their values are. Some people within communities go so far as to say that "knowledge is stories" and that the memory is story based; in other words, while not all memories are stories, understanding in a real sense means correlating the story we are hearing with a story that we already know. The fact that storytelling is one of the oldest and most persistent art forms underscores the significance of storytelling. Thus, the universal appeal of story must be taken into serious consideration by every communicator.³⁴

Everybody's life is full of stories. This enabled Jesus to relate didactically to people; he taught them by means of stories or parables. If one takes a good look at the Synoptic Gospels, it is obvious that they are bursting with parables. Jesus understood the power of story to communicate truth that was usually hard to hear (that is, accept or understand).

Jesus broke new ground in using parables. Jesus' parables were something new, and the people wondered at this new teaching. This new form was indeed story. "Jesus used parables to tell all these things to the crowds; he would not say a thing to them without using a parable" (Matthew 13:34, TEV). Jesus definitely laid the foundation for sound, effective preaching that uses the art of story to convey a powerful message.

Consider the following sermon as an example of preaching *about* a narrative and as a story itself. Evaluate how the preacher sets the stage and defines a conflict to be resolved. The sermon uses imagination expressed through plot, word play, and anecdotes, but the focus remains on the gospel. How might you use your own imagination to write sermons that tell a story?

Sermon *When Jesus Was in the House*

When [Jesus] returned to Capernaum after some days, it was reported that he was at home [in the house]. So many gathered around that there was no longer room for them, not even in front of the door; and he was speaking the word to them. Then some people came, bringing to him a paralyzed man, carried by four of them. And when they could not bring him to Jesus because of the crowd, they removed the roof above him; and after having dug through it, they let down the mat on which the paralytic lay. When Jesus saw their faith, he said to the paralytic, "Son, your sins are forgiven."

—Mark 2:1–5, NRSV

The clamor and the clatter, the jockeying for position—jostling persons to and fro, trying to create a space for ourselves outside someone else's door is strange. And to gather in their front yard is even more of an unusual phenomenon. It sounds so much like the furor and hype over a rock star, a rap artist, a Mick Jagger, a Dr. Dre—you name it, you pick the star! Jesus, you see is at home or, as the King James Version of the Bible says, he's "in the house."

Our houses, whether homes or churches, whether great cathedrals or storefronts, whether duplexes or condominiums, whether Cape Cods or colonials, are often devoid of any spirituality, any inherent transforming elements, anything other than comfort and relaxation. When we return home from someplace, whether our daily jobs or someplace else, we are seeking refuge, solace, trying to get away for a moment's rest, and whether that's the case or not, nobody is really clamoring after us, trying to see us or to hear us, touch us, or feel our presence, unless it's the police or somebody you owe some money gathering around your door to collect. I know if I went home and as soon as I got settled, a whole bunch of folk showed up, I would be a little concerned. Our houses have become havens, places where we can hide and let our hair down, kick off our shoes, soak our feet, watch the game, go to sleep, curl up on the couch, read the newspaper, finish a novel, something curious and exciting. We often want solace, solitude; we don't want to be disturbed—this is our house! We built it with our hands and our money, and we are not going to be bothered by all these strange folk trying to get into the house—

our house, our church, our sanctuary. As a matter of fact, we don't really want these folk, the poor, the paralyzed, the sick, the possessed, the powerless, the paupers—the many.

The many who gathered at the door—multitudes, a whole host of people—heard that Jesus was in the house, so they all came clamoring, closing in on one another, pushing and shoving, trying to get close to him, trying to be touched, trying to hear the teacher, the Son of Man, the one who speaks with authority and conviction and power—the one who forgives sins and heals folk—the one who says in essence that sin and sickness have been forgiven—the debt has been paid, forgiven. Clearly this is what our chosen text conveys—an authoritative forgiveness of a savior. A preacher, a teacher, the Son of Man, the Son of David, the Son of God, Jesus, the personified God, Jesus the exorcist, Jesus the healer.

We are just in the second chapter of the story, and he has already done all of these things. His ministry in Galilee has just begun—the man with the unclean spirit, Simon's mother-in-law, and others sick and possessed, including the leper, have been touched, and now he's back in Capernaum—in the house. Instead of doing what most of us do, he's doing God's will. Yet the reporters are there. The "reporters"—the Bible says, "It was reported that he was at home." The reporters were already there, staked out, and they had gone out and told others.

I don't know who they are in your community or in your church, but somebody is going to report something just like this text says. This report is what we need in our newspapers and magazines—a good one.

We find Jesus doing ministry, proclaiming the word, interpreting the kingdom of God, helping folk—this house has been transformed. It is no longer an ordinary house, no longer just a place to eat and sleep, no longer simply a place to study and play or to dine and recline, no longer a place to watch the news, but it is now where the news is. It is a news station, a place where the Good News is being heard and felt. This house is now the center of attention. It is the main focus of folks flocking from every crevice and corner of the city. This house is surrounded by folk because something different is here. I'm sure there are other houses on the street, in the neighborhood—but this house is unique, it is special, it is different. This house is different, it is special, not because of the way it was designed, not because of its windows and doors, not because it has a trellis here or cornice there. It is special not because of its brick or vinyl, its marble-top vanities and red oak floors—oh, this house is special because Jesus was there. Jesus was in the house. Any house, whether your home, your house, or the church house, whether the sanctuary or education building, whether balcony or in the basement—Jesus is there.

What does it mean for Jesus to be in the house? What does it mean for Jesus to be in the church house? When Jesus is home, when he's in the house, when Jesus comes to Capernaum—when he comes back from the sea, from the boat, from the seashores and goes back to the space that is limited by partitioned walls, limited by windows, ceilings, and roofs—when Jesus is in the house, what does this say to us? Well, come journey with me through the text here in Mark 2:1–12.

First, when Jesus is in the house preaching and speaking, the word takes precedence over the structure of the building. Preaching the word becomes primary. It is evident that this house that Jesus was in is too small for the crowd. Even the yard out front, near the door could not contain the throng of folk seeking to hear the word. This scene reminds me of the house church we had growing up in central Virginia. We would go to my grandmother's house to hear one of my uncle's friends preach. We would set up chairs in the house, on the porch, and in the yard to hear what thus says the Lord! When Jesus is in the house, the Word will be spoken. In this case, he is the embodiment of the word, and the word embodies his purpose. When Jesus is in the house, the word will be preached and taught. The ways of God will be shared. Jesus was in the house speaking the word, telling a parable, sharing a story, prophesying, trying to help folk understand who he was and what his purpose was. He is at home, in the house, in Capernaum, where the opposition to him mounts and his enemies are always on the watch; they too are in the crowd, in the yard, on the porch—in the house, and Jesus is preaching the word. A word that is not necessarily what they want to hear, but what God wants them to hear, a word that strikes at their tradition, their legalism, their ideas and practices. This word that Jesus is speaking has power to propel folk into believing, and to prompt them to put in practice the purpose of God—yes, the word, embodying Jesus' own purpose, helps folk to understand the power of God.

The word, this word comes alive in Jesus. This word Jesus is speaking is about God—it is about himself. The word speaks of God, the mercy of God, the wisdom of God; the word . . . "In the beginning . . . the Word was with God, and the Word was God" (John 1:1, NRSV). "I treasure your word in my heart, so that I may not sin against you" (Psalm 119:11, NRSV). The word has power in season and out of season. Jesus is also the Word, the embodiment of the Word, the personified Word, the living Word, the teaching Word, the healing Word! Jesus is in the house speaking the word to them.

Oh, we must preach the word! In the church, the word will be spoken! When Jesus is in the church house, this word, this *logos*, this powerful, potent, prevailing, penetrating, precious word—cutting left and right, convincing and converting us, helping and healing us, even haunting us when we do wrong—yes, when Jesus is in the church house, the word will be heard.

Second, this text teaches us that when Jesus is in the house, extreme measures, drastic measures will sometimes need to be taken. In other words, you may have to tear the roof off the house—off the church, if that is what it takes to get to Jesus. People on the outside and on the inside knew Jesus was there and probably heard him, and the text says, "Some people came"—a group of them—"bringing to him a paralyzed man, carried by four of them." And the crowd was so intense, so compact that they could not get the man to Jesus, so they took the roof off the house—right above where Jesus was speaking—and they put the mat and the man through the roof and laid him down where Jesus was.

We can't allow anything—not the crowd, not the steps, not the stone or the straw, nothing in the house, outside the house, or on top of the house—whether it's a hip roof, an A roof, a cedar shake roof, an asphalt roof, a slate roof, a flat roof, a built-up roof—nothing should keep us from Jesus. Sometimes folk in the church will "blow the roof off the place"; you have to take drastic action, go to the extreme, be unconventional, do what's necessary and not worry about the crowd, don't be intimidated by the crowd, don't let the crowd, the multitude, folk from all over standing in front of the door get between you and Jesus. Charles Tindley had the right idea: "Nothing between my soul and the Savior, so that His blessed face be seen; nothing preventing the least of his favor, keep the way clear! Let nothing between." Don't let anything get in the way.

We are living in some rough times today, paralyzed by the shock and horror of murder. Oh, yes, we are in Capernaum, we have our own Palestine—places where the faithful people of God need to get to Jesus—yes, whether it is Los Angeles or Washington, D.C., whether it is Norfolk or Richmond, or even Union, South Carolina, or some other little town, we have some folk who are sick, plainly possessed by paralyzing force that needs to be healed. Right here in this church and in other churches, we need to do some drastic things to get folk to Jesus. We got some folk who are broken today, those who are hurt, those who are suffering from all kinds of diseases, broken by the hurt that comes from families and friends—paralyzed by the dependency on drugs, parents and grandparents who are afraid of their own children—oh, yes, there is a powerful paralysis that's present in the land, yet somebody has to be bold enough to take extreme measures, bold enough to help pick each other up and take us to Jesus. You may have to cut a hole in the roof, but that's all right! If that's what it takes to get to Jesus, then that is what we will do!

Finally, when Jesus is in the house, forgiveness and healing will take place. Notice that while the scribes are questioning in their hearts, thinking to themselves, Jesus asks, "Which is easier, to say . . . 'Your sins are forgiven,' or . . . 'Stand up and take your mat and walk'?" (verse 9, NRSV). Jesus forgives the man's sins, and his healing becomes a demonstration or a consequence of his forgiveness. Oh, the scribes are upset; these doctors of the law are disturbed. They are frantic and furious because this man has got to be crazy to speak as if he is God. This is blasphemy! Well, because Jesus knows who he is, because he is the Son of God and the Son of Man, because he can fully relate to God and man, and because he is fully God and fully man, he has the power to forgive sins and to heal sickness. Jesus can do it.

Some are holding grudges from the sixties and seventies—mad with folk, harboring hatred in our hearts; Jesus has already forgiven and healed them. You see, there is a connection between faith, forgiveness, and healing. When Jesus is in the house, not only does it become a church, a sanctuary where the word is heard and preached, where people are taught about the ways of God and the need for boldness and drastic action on the part of the faithful, but when Jesus is in the house, the church can even be a healing station—a hospital, if you will. In this story, Jesus heals the man who was paralyzed, and he can heal you and me. When Jesus is in the house, the physician, the doctor is in. Oh, he doesn't need a scalpel, no need for a stethoscope, no need for any stitches; he won't need anesthesia. The house is his operating room; the church house is his recovery room. When Jesus is in the house, all you need is a touch; when Jesus is in the house, all you need is for him to speak. Your sins are forgiven; rise, take up your bed, and walk. When Jesus is in the house, the faithful gather around the door. The weak and strong can come; the poor, the disenfranchised, the dispossessed can come. When Jesus is in the house, the paralyzed, the sick, the lame can be healed.

6

Preaching Plainly:
How to Put the Sermon Together—
The Harris Method

> Preachers have to learn how to live in eternity, while in the
> midst of time.
> —Samuel DeWitt Proctor
>
> We are called upon to wrestle with a great idea.
> —Howard Thurman

Preaching good sermons that are tightly constructed is a difficult and continuous process that requires a broad understanding of people, coupled with knowledge of the biblical text and the concerns and needs of the congregation. We need to know why and what to do in order to put together a sermon that speaks to the heart and soul of folk who come to church week after week in order to "hear a word" from the Lord. This is an awesome responsibility for which none of us has been adequately prepared.

Preaching remains the heart and soul of the church. This "two-edged sword" represents the value and importance of the sermon. Preaching does indeed cut both ways, left and right. By this, I mean that the real and the ideal are encountered and affected by the sermon. The sermon is not only able to cut out the mess that exists in the lives of folk who flock to hear the word, but in doing so, it heals the wounds of those who have been hurt by the painful blows of life. The sermon is more than a salve or topical ointment; it is a transforming instrument—a scalpel, a sword, indeed, a two-edged sword that cuts in both directions so that it gets to the heart of the matter, penetrating to the core where the essence of one's life is affected and where hope can be restored, rejuvenated, and rekindled. The writer of the book of Hebrews makes this convincingly clear with the following words: "The word of God is living and active, sharper than any two-edged sword, piercing until it divides soul from spirit, joints from marrow; it is able to judge the thoughts and intentions of the heart" (Hebrews 4:12, NRSV).

Preaching and Worship

Every worship experience in the church demands preparation and planning. There are many liturgical considerations, particular traditions, and other relevant concerns that must be examined before we sing the hymn of praise or utter the invocation. Nevertheless, it is the preaching moment that remains at the center of most worship experiences, whether it's Thanksgiving Day, Unity Sunday, Christmas, or an occasion such as a funeral. Preaching is central particularly in the African American Church. Melva Wilson Costen makes this point clear:

> "Is there a word from the Lord?" This question, which was embedded in the souls of the slaves, continues with African worshipers. For some, all of the other elements are preliminary to the preached word. This confirms the importance and centrality of preaching [in] Black worship from the Invisible Institution to the present.[1]

There is general agreement among churchgoers that preaching is at the center of contextual religious practice. In the following pages, I try to demonstrate that, regardless of the occasion, the demands of the sermon are the same. The preacher is called to be an interpreter during special occasions as well as general worship. The struggle is to refrain from succumbing to the overwhelming lure of the occasion to preempt the development of the biblical text. This means that the preacher must thoroughly integrate the demands of the context and occasion with the chosen text and not allow the occasion and its history to become canonized as if it were text. Special occasions are challenging to the preacher because there is an effort to address the special circumstances of worship without compromising the interpretation of the text in the preaching event.

The Word Made Plain

We live in a word-infested world. These words are not always encouraging and enlightening, not always exciting and enlivening, not always enriching and empowering, but sometimes they are empty and envious, encircling our experiences of joy with ugly expressions of enmity and evil and hate. The words that people use, the things that people say to us and about us can do good or harm. These words can build up or tear down; they can create hope and love, or they can cause fear and despair. We really should watch and weigh what we say to folk, how we relate to them with words. In this connection, profanity can be a problem. It doesn't take much creativity or verbal skill to use profanity—to use God's name in vain, to call someone an expletive, or to refer disparagingly to someone else. There are those who don't do extremely well on the verbal part of the SAT or the GRE, the GMAT or the LSAT, but can score high on the test of expletives, cussing skills that have been glamorized by many rappers who are financed by large record companies and other money moguls.

I used to think—naively—that girls and women didn't use profanity, but recently, as I had finished conducting a funeral service at the gravesite and after the interment, I could hear in the distance rumblings of rank language getting closer and closer to my ears. Two women were doing some low-down, drill sergeant, naval-base-like cussing! If you can imagine it, they were saying it, gesturing or gesticulating toward each other, threatening to fight. They were using fighting words— words that could create potentially violent behavior right there in the cemetery. I was praying that I would not have to witness this tragic act of black-on-black crime, this anger spill over into a physical altercation. Then I noticed something that I could hardly believe—that they all, one by one, got into the same car and drove off together. I was astonished, yet pleased that the exchange of words did not lead to disaster. Our words are often harmful and hurtful. They are sometimes jagged and jeering and jarring. They can belittle, or they can build up and encourage liberation and transformation.

Conversely, the word of God is more powerful than our unsanctified words. The aforesaid scripture (Hebrews 4:12) is couched in the middle of the writer's sermon on rest for the people of God (Hebrews 3:1–4:13). However, the word represents the closing of that sermon. It is the conclusion written in what Thomas Long calls "time honored homiletical fashion"; the preacher wraps up this message with a tribute to the power of God's word. The word of God is alive and active. Its power is not dormant or sedentary, but alive, full of verve and nerve, full of power and strength, full of virtue and victory. The word of God is active and alive—working deep in the heart and mind—working on our conscience—constructing a new understanding of our relationship with one another and with God. In sharing the word through preaching and teaching, we hope to make God's word an active, powerful vehicle addressing some of life's issues in a cutting-edge way.

The image and metaphor of the sermon—the word of God as a two-edged sword—captures the hyperbolic nature of the language and practice of preaching. This language is imaginative and picturesque, a necessary stylistic ingredient in the preaching moment. This word must be plainly spoken, taking into consideration the scriptural text and the congregation as text, as well as its context.

The Preacher and the Biblical and Congregational Text

The biblical text and the African American experience are the Black preacher's main tools for expounding on the word of God. The context and the experiences of the preacher play a role in the understanding and interpretation of the text. The text is not an old, isolated relic of the past that is irrelevant to the needs of today. It does, however, need to be interpreted and reinterpreted for the community in which it is being used. This means that the preacher must ferret out of the text its meaning for people who seek to be scriptural—that is, biblical and, more precisely, textual—forgoing the precarious prating and prattling of the comic or comedian who often mimics the preacher as a verbose, empty talker. This popular culture caricature of the Black preacher by actors and comedians such as Cedric the Entertainer and Bernie Mac does a disservice to the serious and competent heralders of the gospel.

Textual preaching—choosing a text, developing a subject based on the chosen text, and then proceeding to develop the text in all of its fluidity and complexity—is the most essential requirement for preaching. Preaching, then, must be textual and contextual because the transformative power of the sermon is grounded in the biblical text, not in the topic, but in the real-life situation as correlated or contrasted with the ideal of the scriptural text. The topic is not the text. One cannot disconnect the text from the subject. The text is the mother of the subject or title. The text gives birth to the subject. Too often the preacher will choose a text as a pretext and pretense to the real development of the scriptural text. The preacher will read the text to the congregation as the basis of the sermon and then proceed to pretend to develop the text, but will in fact develop a topic that often is out of synchrony with the chosen text. The development of a topic is quite often not indicative of the preacher's ability, but is usually more expedient than wrestling with the scriptural text. Making the sermon relevant and real to the church of today requires some hermeneutical skills and stick-to-itiveness on the part of the preacher.

The power of the sermon is also grounded in the preacher's commitment to struggle with the text and allow the text to speak for itself and to address the needs of the congregation. When the preacher allows the text to speak, it will speak words of wisdom and comfort, love and compassion, freedom and hope, redemption and salvation to a faithless generation—a world in need of transformation. The sermon and the points or moves must flow from the text itself and not simply from general biblical literature, history, or sociology. So the text must be read and re-read over and over until it can be correlated with the context and until it is absorbed into the preacher's consciousness. This absorption enables the preacher to interpret the text in a new language that the people can understand.

The Context: The Local Church

The preacher mainly speaks in the local congregation where he or she has at least a weekly opportunity to share the word of God with the people of God. While not all preaching is done in the local church, the church remains the most visible and viable institution where the gospel can be developed and heard. Moreover, the embodiment of the gospel in the lives of church folk remains a critical goal and objective of the sermon.

The sermon is the means by which persons are encouraged to embody forgiveness, love, prudence, peace, justice, and faith. The local church is the harbinger of our faith commitment. It is the locus of training in Christian teachings and principles, thereby serving as the incubator and nurturer of the virtues heretofore mentioned. Many of us first learned to speak before a group in our local congregations. Also, children were taught to recite and memorize scripture, to participate in theater groups, to work together and display the attributes of Christian teachings in their daily lives. The local church is the place where we first learned to become the people of God as an extension of our very being. There can be no discussion that takes seriously the whole of African American culture without understanding that the Black church and Black religion are critical components of our culture and history.

Developing the Sermon

Sermon points, as African American preachers continue to describe them, or moves, as David Buttrick has described,[2] are somewhat like pieces of a puzzle. A single piece of the puzzle does not represent the whole, but once the pieces are connected to each other, they become a whole picture, something recognizable, something that the eye and mind are able to identify. Therefore, points are not randomly selected, but rather carefully extrapolated from the chosen biblical text in order that they might be integrated into the development of the sermon. Carefully extrapolating one's point from the chosen text eliminates the mistaken notion that points can be gotten from anywhere or that the effort is limited to placing pretty words together, such as alliteration that often finds no foundation or credence in the selected text.

A thorough understanding of the text and one's own context will help assure that points are extracted from the selected biblical text. Points are not simply general or topical in terms of the Bible referencing them in many places. They should be specific! This means that one can locate the point in the selected text, which gives opportunity for the explication of the text rather than the entire Bible, from Genesis to Revelation.

The burden is upon the preacher to establish a clear picture in his or her mind before submitting this picture to the hearer or congregation. These sermon points can be tested, as we shall see later. This clear picture allows the preacher to formulate an outline that will help to shape the sermon by developing a strong point to be readily grasped and understood by the congregation. This involves some imagination on the part of the preacher and the congregation.

After a clear picture is produced, based on the selected text and then further broken down into points, subpoints, or moves, it becomes necessary that the preacher explain what each point means, based on the selected text. Making the sermon relevant and contemporary is critical to understanding the gospel nature of preaching. Preaching the gospel is a process of relating an old text in a new way to a new generation. This is the challenge and the joy of putting the sermon together.

But how is this done? Share with the congregation where the point or major move is located in the selected text. Points ideally should come directly from the text, not in the exact language of the text, but a translated, contemporary interpretation of the text. Sometimes these points are explicit, and at other times a case may be made from what is implied in the text or what the preacher infers from reading the selected text. By all means, make transparent to the hearer what captured your attention in the text and enabled you to extrapolate this particular point from the chosen text, and how it became clear to you, the preacher. Feel free to allow the listener to follow you by repeatedly telling the congregation which scriptural verse or verses the point comes from within the selected text. This allows the listener to participate with the preacher as he or she connects the pieces of the unfolding elements of the sermon.

Substantiate the sermon's point primarily by using the information embedded in the selected text. Supportive information from other biblical or literary references can sometimes prove helpful or hazardous. This does not mean that the preacher should avoid using other references, but they should be used with precision and some degree of caution. Preachers often clutter their sermons with extraneous material that fails to clarify a point or move. This material then becomes a mere digression, an aside or deviation from the meaning and intent, and does not enhance the sermon. This often causes the listener to become uninterested or unable to adequately follow or to see clearly the picture the preacher is trying to paint with words. The use of literature, history, poetry, stories, and real-life examples and experiences can help to make the point more vivid (see "Illustrations," later in this chapter).

Repetition

Restating the point of the text by using phrases such as *in other words, simply stated,* or *allow me to be redundant* is a way of repeating what was said in another way for impact and memorization—often in the language of the masses or the common vernacular. This can make plain the point the preacher is trying to construct. Repetition of the main point is an easy linguistic tool used to help your congregation retain what you have deemed important. This can be done without the use of excessive verbiage, which is a burden the preacher must constantly struggle to avoid.

This does not suggest that the listener lacks intelligence; on the contrary, restating your point is a way of reinforcing that which has already been stated. It is not an attempt to introduce something new. Moreover, it gives the listener who didn't hear or comprehend fully what was previously stated an opportunity to hear again that which is important to the preacher's development of the sermon.

This is a form of reiteration, not verboseness. It is an attempt to clarify and saturate the hearer with different ways of hearing and understanding the same information, with the ultimate goal of clarity. The preacher is trying to help each hearer come to the point of saying, "I see!" "Aha!" Repetition is a literary and rhetorical tool used to impress meaning upon the mind of the hearer. Repetition should be used without being redundant. Repetition is an important homiletical tool that does not always mean redundancy. It is an affective and effective component of the preaching task.

Explicating the Text

Explicating or explaining a point means using language that enables the listener to find his or her place in the story as the sermon unfolds. Too often in the church, points are made, but the hearer interprets them as applying to someone else—especially other church members. It is the preacher's responsibility to aim the gospel message directly at the individual listener and at himself or herself. This helps to assure that all parishioners will recognize or feel that the sermon is addressed personally to them. The preacher is compelled to use his or her best resources to create a kinship with the hearer that allows each person in the congregation to feel and say that this sermon "speaks directly or indirectly to me, either where I am now or where I once was or maybe where I will be someday." The preacher must understand that not everyone in the congregation will experience the same things at the same time or in the same manner. However, at some point, each individual will find him- or herself in one of these categories.

When developing points, the conscientious preacher keeps in mind the three categories listed in order to reach as many persons as possible. Most folk come to church to be helped in their daily lives, with the expectation that the preacher will say something to help them interpret their particular experiences in a way that enables them to face the present and future with renewed hope and faith. The preacher is compelled via the sermon to help folk face life-and-death issues in a way that others are either unable or unwilling to do.

Before going any further, the preacher must wrestle with the text for a sustained period of time. This means that the preacher must do the following as preparation for writing the textual sermon:

1. Choose the scriptural text before stating a proposition.

2. Extrapolate a sermon title from the chosen text. Allow the title of the sermon to flow from the text. This demands a sustained practice of study, prayer, fasting, and imagination. By imagination, I mean that the preacher should not be too restrained or restricted by the past or dominant interpretations, but should allow him- or herself to be lured into the realm of possibilities, where the future of the text's meaning is more promising than the past or, as Paul Ricoeur says, "The meaning of the text is in front of it," not behind it. To be able to settle on a sermon title, the preacher may have to go through a process of eliminating sermon titles that don't quite work as well as others. It is not unusual to have three to five possible titles before settling on the "best one."

3. After settling on the best title as a result of reading and rereading the text in several translations and then memorizing it in your own words, you are ready to write the proposition. The proposition is a short statement that gives direction to the sermon. It serves to focus the preacher on the ultimate meaning of the text in a succinct, albeit sentential form. This sentence should be the road map for constructing the sermon. The proposition is a proposal; it is a plan, a structural diagram of what the sermon is about. Every sermon needs a proposition. However, before one can write the proposition, one has to do some exegetical and hermeneutical work. This involves

defining and understanding the meaning of every word in the chosen text. If you know the original languages, this will help you to relate the meaning to the current interpretation so that the difference and distance between then and now can be bridged.

4. Now it is time to get started with the introduction of the sermon. Inasmuch as the textual exegesis has been done, the contextual analysis has been comprehended. You can begin the introduction with a current situation that can be correlated with the text. This can be a story grounded in life experience or an interpretation of a life event that is informed by the chosen text.

After the introduction, which should be only about one or two typed pages, develop the body of the sermon based on the chosen text and the exegesis of the congregation. The body should be about three typed pages. A five- to six-page typed manuscript (in twelve-point font) is enough to keep the preacher in the pulpit for fifteen to eighteen minutes. After this, the preacher is ready to sit down! And the congregation is also ready for him or her to bring the sermon to a close.

Illustrations

Many resources are available to preachers for illustrating the sermon. First and foremost is personal experience, which includes but is not limited to that which we have witnessed, read about, and felt. The preacher can also use the experiences of others. As I have suggested, there are books that contain thousands of illustrations, stories, histories, philosophies, etc. that may be used at will. Illustrations also take the form of poetry and popular songs that we hear; movies, fables, or tales that are told; and carefully crafted stories and personal experiences.

Illustrations, when properly used, can raise the sermon point to a new level. Choosing the most helpful illustration is an awesome responsibility because its purpose is to create and enhance a kinship to the listener. Illustrations provide the perfect opportunity for the preacher to make his or her point clear. The sermon illustration is the final chance to make plain that which the preacher has been saying since stating, restating, and explaining the point. Its purpose is to drive the point home in a thoroughly clear and picturesque way that could not have been accomplished in either of the prior ways of stating it. The illustration has a life of its own and often serves as a parabolic way of making the point plain and simple. That's why it is so necessary to harness and use it effectively. People often leave church impressed by the illustration that was heard without realizing that it was simply a vehicle to clarify the point the preacher was making. It is the final attempt to make plain and portable the essence of the sermon. Good illustrations are some of the most helpful tools at the preacher's disposal, but to use them precisely, the preacher must be a reader with a broad array of interests such as history, literature, biography, art, philosophy, music, theology, sociology, and science.

Finally, as preachers of the gospel, we have to be careful that we do not make one point from the text and erroneously illustrate another. This not only will confound the hearer, but also will undo whatever good the sermon had previously done! A bad illustration is worse than no illustration at all. And a good illustration is worth more than a thousand words.

This final sermon was written using the principles explained in this chapter. As you read it, look for language that is both imaginative and plain, as well as for a message that is "portable" and relevant to a modern congregation. Also look for places where the preacher restates main points for emphasis and explicates the text. Can you find yourself in this sermon? What elements of the "Harris method" might improve your own sermons?

Sermon *A Question of Identity—Chaos, Self, and Other*

> One day [Jesus] got into a boat with his disciples, and he said to them, "Let us go across to the other side of the lake." So they put out, and while they were sailing he fell asleep. A windstorm swept down on the lake, and the boat was filling with water, and they were in danger. They went to him and woke him up, shouting, "Master, Master, we are perishing!" And he woke up and rebuked the wind and the raging waves; they ceased, and there was a calm. He said to them, "Where is your faith?" They were afraid and amazed, and said to one another, "Who then is this, that he commands even the winds and the water, and they obey him?"
>
> —Luke 8:22–25, NRSV

Chaos seems to be a ubiquitous presence, a pandemic phenomenon seen vividly in a storm, in a conflict—in the physical universe and in the social order, in the republic, in the nation, and in the hearts and minds of individuals. Chaos is a state of confusion and disorder. It is unclarity or the lack of focus and direction. Chaos seems to be everywhere—in foreign policy, in public policy, and in government, national and local.

Noam Chomsky, the internationally acclaimed linguistics philosopher and scholar, says, "The primary concern of US foreign policy is to guarantee the freedom to rob and exploit."[3] Consider Iraq. The United States provided Iraq with weapons and materials of terror during Iraq's war with Iran. Now we're acting like terrorism is only practiced by other nations, when we ourselves have terrorized smaller nation-states and persons within our own borders, like African Americans from the seventeenth century until the present time. Who was it that enslaved a whole race of people while writing treatises on freedom and justice? Who was it that talked about democracy and human rights while simultaneously denying Blacks and women the right to vote? Who was it that put a reward on the head of two conductors of the Underground Railroad, Harriet Tubman and Sojourner Truth? Black people have been terrorized long before the recent preoccupation with terrorism by Democrats and Republicans, by federalists and the states' rights advocates, by the Jeffersonians and James Monroes—by the night riders and the Ku Klux Klansmen, by the staunch segregationists and the gradualists. So whether it's about the balance of power in the U.S. Senate or the election of a mayor in Richmond, Virginia, chaos seems to be the order of the day.

In the cities people are being murdered, shot in the head and wrapped in plastic bags and dumped in the open street, in the alley, in the Dumpster—anywhere. Children are being murdered by strangers as well as by their own mothers and fathers. Others are being abused by moral leaders and teachers. The schools and the neighborhoods are often like war zones. People are being randomly shot and murdered by strangers who have gone on a psychotic murderous rampage. Chaos and conflict, chaos and disorder have frightened and caused fear and faithlessness everywhere. And so today, there are many who can readily identify with the reality and the spirit of this text in the Gospel of Luke.

There is a striking difference between the attitude, the demeanor, and the behavior of Jesus and that of his disciples. They are overcome by terror—terrorized by the wind and the waves and the water, and Jesus is engulfed by the tranquil and peaceful posture of sleep. Jesus is calm, as evidenced by his sleep. Jesus is resting in the peace of God, while the disciples are terrified, also by the power of God. For Jesus, the nature of God is one of peaceful tranquility; for the disciples, God creates fear.

The contrast in their reactions is due to their different under-standings of who God is. Jesus recognizes and knows who is in control of the universe, so he goes to sleep. He absolutely con-nects with God; he trusts God. He understands who God is as Creator. Yet the disciples understand neither God, nor the Son of God, Jesus Christ, Savior and Lord. Why else would they be in such a tizzy, such a frenzy, such a torrid and totalizing ter-ror, causing them to totter on the brink of anguish and anxiety? They say, "Jesus, we are going under. We are about to perish." They are flat-out fearful and scared. They have panicked, shouting, "Wake up! Master, master, we are perishing!"

The truth is that they were in worse danger before the storm than they are in now. They just did not recognize it or know it. It is not the storm that puts them in a dangerous position, but their own lack of faith, their lack of understanding who Jesus is. They were in danger, but not necessarily from this storm, because Jesus is in fact on the boat. God can and does bring order out of chaos.

This story identifies Jesus with God. The incarnation is evi-dent here. "God was in Christ," as D. M. Baillie attests. Jesus "woke up and rebuked the wind and the raging waves; they ceased, and there was a calm" (verse 24). This chaos repre-sented by the stormy, angry sea is subject to the power of Jesus. Jesus restores order to primordial chaos, just as God did in Genesis 1.

But more importantly, the stormy sea and the chaotic waters reflected the disciples' inner chaos—their inability to recognize who Jesus is. You see, even the wind and waves obey him, yet the disciples don't really know him and don't adhere to his teaching. The water, the raging sea, the deluge and the demons, Hurricane Isidore and Hurricane Lili cannot resist the power of God. Leprosy, disease—the blind are given sight, the lame walk, and those with diseases are healed. Even the dead are brought to life by his authority and by his power, and yet the disciples disobey him. They did not do what they had heard. His word had not taken root in their hearts and souls, so they did not know calmness; they did not know peace and trust. When the waves and wind could obey his will, the disciples could not.

Why is it that moving from chaos to calmness is not enough? First, when the storm is over, we are still not satisfied, not convinced about ourselves or our Savior. There is a lingering identification with chaos. It seems to me that we have to stop being in complicity with the chaos.

The disciples identify with chaos. Their terror and faithlessness suggest their propensity to be in solidarity with chaos. And we have folk like that in the church and in the community. As long as there is a storm, as long as there is something going on to cause tension and terror and chaos, these folk are fine. Their self-understanding, their practices of faith and ministry are grounded in chaos. Some folk are not satisfied by peace and tranquility and will not rest until they can find something to identify with—chaos in family, chaos in church, chaos in community. We are indeed like the "disciples of Jesus" because we identify with their faults, failures, and faithlessness. We identify more with them than we do with Jesus. We have a disciples theology.

Then Jesus asked the disciples, "Where is your faith?" The scripture text says, "They were afraid and amazed." Second, moving from chaos to calmness is not enough because we have to get to the point of faith. The absence of faith remains a residual even after the storm has obediently responded to the voice and power of God. The text says that Jesus rebuked or ordered the wind and waves to stop. The power of the word is reflected in Jesus' speech to the physical elements—the wind and the waves calming down in absolute obedience to his will. This is further evidence of the incarnation that the disciples completely missed. Jesus then asked, "Where is your faith?

Don't you have any faith? If you have faith, where is it? Has it sunk to the bottom of the sea, or has the wind blown your faith into oblivion? Where is your faith? Where is your understanding of the power of God? And who do you understand yourself to be?" Self-understanding always occurs through understanding something other than the self. Where is your faith? How are you going to be able to preach and teach, to tell the story of your experience, your relationship with the Son of God, the Son of Man and the Son of David? Notice now that the storm is over, and everything should be back to normal. But the text says that the preresponse to Jesus' question was that they were "afraid and amazed."

Notice the correlation: they were afraid and amazed. They were disturbed and apprehensive on the one hand, and confused and stunned and astonished on the other. This calming of the storm, this cessation of chaos creates fear, because while they had maybe a little understanding of how the sea, the wind, and the waves were subject to erratic and unruly action and behavior, their understanding of Jesus is less clear because Jesus is more powerful than the storm. Instead of bringing calmness and comfort to the disciples, being in Jesus' presence creates fear and amazement.[4] And they said to one another, "Who then is this, that he commands even the winds and the water, and they obey him?" (verse 25). Who then is this? Who is this? What a question! They still do not know him after he has transformed chaos into calm. The sea is no longer raging, and the winds have ceased. The trouble is over, yet they ask, "Who then is he?"

Finally, moving from chaos to calmness is not enough because the identity question is still hanging out there: Who is Jesus? Who then is this? Jesus has commanded that chaos to cease. Jesus has spoken, and the wind and the sea have been made mute. Jesus' speech has obviated the outspoken, howling, and boisterous sounds of the wind and the waves. Jesus is the voice, the speech, the *logos* and power of God. This event, like all events, would vanish—pass away like the withering of grass or the fading of flowers—but how this event is understood, what this event means becomes the foundation, the starting point, the embryonic foundation for proclaiming the Gospel. Their question to each other, though grounded in a thick disconnect and distance between them and Jesus, nevertheless is a question that must be answered. This is indeed a very relevant question!

Your family is well. Your children are all healthy and safe. You have been in the hospital, and now you are back home. You have had surgery, and now you are on the mend. You can walk again, you have the use of your limbs, and you are in your right mind, your speech is no longer slurred, your family is doing well. The doctor has given you a clean bill of health. You have a job, and your bills are paid. The storm is over, and you are still asking, "Who is this that commands the winds and the waves, and they obey?"

I have a certain vagueness, a certain denseness, certain questions of understanding and misunderstanding that linger in mind. I may not fully understand Schleiermacher, Kant, or Heidegger. I may not understand abstract analytical philosophy as well as I should, but on the question of who then is this, I have come to say in the language of the Black preacher, "If you don't know who woke you up this morning and who put food on your table, if you don't know who worked a miracle in your life—who took the taste of alcohol from your lips, who stopped you from drinking and driving and saved you from yourself; if you don't know today who picked you up and turned your life around, let me assure you that it was not Sigmund Freud or Carl Jung or Dr. Phil. It was not your id or ego or superego. It was not the palm reader or the soothsayer. It was not your own frail and weak wisdom. It was not your family, and it was not your economic status." Who then is this who has created a sense of wholeness in your mind and in your body? Who then is this who has calmed your fears and brought serenity and peace to your life? Who then is this?

The text doesn't say, but can I answer for the doubting disciples? Can I answer for the ones who have been to the "mourners' bench," those who have been baptized, those "who have come a mighty long way," those who are afraid to speak, those who are still unable to recognize the power and presence of God? Who then is this? His name is Jesus. Who then is this? He is Messiah; he is King of Kings, Lord of Lords. He is Isaiah's comforter and Mark's messianic secret. He is John's revelation and Paul's message of grace.

Notes

Preface

1. C. Eric Lincoln and Lawrence H. Mamiya, *The Black Church in the African American Experience* (Durham, NC: Duke University Press, 1990), 411.

2. Aldon D. Morris, *The Origins of the Civil Rights Movement: Black Communities Organizing for Change* (New York: Free Press, 1984), 5.

1. The Preacher's Self-Understanding

1. Carl G. Jung, *The Undiscovered Self* (New York: American Library, 1957).

2. See David F. Ford, *Self and Salvation: Being Transformed* (Cambridge: Cambridge University Press, 1999), 19.

3. Martin Luther King Jr., *Where Do We Go from Here: Chaos or Community?* (New York: Harper and Row, 1967), 40.

4. Ibid., 41.

5. Ibid.

6. Ibid., 43.

7. Ibid., 43–44.

8. Boykin Sanders, *Blowing the Trumpet in Open Court: Prophetic Judgment and Liberation* (Trenton, N.J.: Africa World Press, 2002), 129.

9. King, *Where Do We Go from Here,* 37.

10. Paul Tillich, *Love, Power, and Justice: Ontological Analysis and Ethical Applications* (London: Oxford University Press, 1954), 25–26.

11. Martin Luther King Jr., "Letter from the Birmingham City Jail," in *A Testament of Hope: The Essential Writings of Martin Luther King Jr.,* ed. James M. Washington (New York: Harper and Row, 1986), 298.

12. Ibid., 299.

13. Ibid.

14. Ibid., 300.

15. Ibid.

16. Ibid., 299.

17. William Desmond, *Being and the Between* (Albany: State University of New York Press, 1995), 417.

18. Charles Marsh, "Christ as the Mediation of the Other," in *Reclaiming Dietrich Bonhoeffer: The Promise of His Theology* (New York: Oxford University Press, 1994), 83–84.

19. Desmond, *Being and the Between*, 386.

20. Ibid., 390.

21. See Hannah Arendt, *The Human Condition* (Chicago: University of Chicago Press, 1958), 159–67.

22. See Brian K. Blount, *Then the Whisper Put On Flesh: New Testament Ethics in an African American Context* (Nashville: Abingdon, 2001).

23. Desmond, *Being and the Between*, 390–91.

24. See the *Norfolk Journal and Guide*, January 2003.

25. King, "Letter," 299.

2. The Preaching of the Elders: Princes of the African American Pulpit

1. John Malcus Ellison, *They Who Preach* (Nashville: Broadman, 1956), 17.

2. Ibid., 2–3.

3. Ibid., 3.

4. Ibid., 9.

5. Ibid., 10.

6. Ibid., 19.

7. Ibid., 11.

8. Ibid.

9. Ibid., 11–12.

10. Samuel D. Proctor, *The Certain Sound of the Trumpet: Crafting a Sermon of Authority* (Valley Forge: Judson Press, 1994), 112–13.

11. Samuel D. Proctor, *The Substance of Things Hoped For: A Memoir of African-American Faith* (Valley Forge: Judson Press, 1999), 40–41.

12. Ibid.

13. Proctor, *Certain Sound of the Trumpet*, 98.

14. Miles Jerome Jones, Annotated Bibliography, class notes (Virginia Union University: PT 533 Introduction to Homiletics, 2001).

15. James M. Wall, "The Sermon: A Work of Art," *The Christian Ministry* 7/6 (November 1976): 28.

16. Paul Tillich, *Love, Power, and Justice* (London: Oxford University Press, 1954), 110.

17. Ibid., 108.

18. See Dietrich Bonhoeffer, *Act and Being: Transcendental Philosophy and Ontology in Systematic Theology*, Dietrich Bonhoeffer Works vol.

2, trans. H. Martin Rumscheidt, ed. Wayne Whitsun Floyd (Minneapolis: Fortress Press, 1996).

19. Tillich, *Love, Power, and Justice*, 25.

20. Ibid.

21. Miles Jerome Jones, class notes (Virginia Union University: PT 533 Introduction to Homiletics, September 12, 2001).

22. Ibid.

23. Ibid.

24. Ibid.

25. Wall, "The Sermon," 28.

26. Jones, September 12, 2001.

27. Ibid.

28. See Paul Ricoeur, *One Self as Another* (Chicago: University of Chicago Press, 1992).

29. Ibid.

30. Jones, September 12, 2001.

31. Ibid.

32. Ibid.

33. Richard Lischer, *The Preacher King: Martin Luther King Jr. and the Word That Moved America* (New York: Oxford University Press, 1995), 201.

34. Ibid.

35. Ibid.

36. Jones, September 12, 2001.

37. Ibid.

38. Miles Jones made these statements during a dialogue and discussion about his method of teaching, "Introduction to Preaching," Virginia Union University, November 2002.

39. Ibid.

40. Ibid.

41. Ibid.

3. The Sermon as Interpretation

1. Mikhail M. Bakhtin, *The Dialogic Imagination: Four Essays*, edited by Michael Holquist, translated by Caryl Emerson and Michael Holquist (Austin: University of Texas Press 1981), 262–63.

2. Alfred North Whitehead, *Process and Reality: An Essay in Cosmology* (New York: Free Press, 1978), 182.

3. Paul Ricoeur, *The Symbolism of Evil* (Boston: Beacon Press, 1967), 347–57.

4. See Whitehead, *Process and Reality*, 121–22.

5. See Mark D. Nanos, *The Mystery of Romans: The Jewish Context of Paul's Letter* (Minneapolis: Fortress Press, 1996), 85–165.

6. Mikhail M. Bakhtin, *Dialogic Imagination*, 259.

7. Ibid., 258.

8. Ibid., 262–63.

9. Ibid., 264.

10. Ibid., 282.

11. Ibid., 282.

12. Ibid., 282.

13. Jacques Derrida, *Monolingualism of the Other or the Prosthesis of Origin* (Stanford: Stanford University Press, 1998), 2.

14. Ibid., 8.

15. Ibid., 25.

16. Martha Nussbaum, *Love's Knowledge: Essays on Philosophy and Literature* (Oxford: Oxford University Press, 1990), 5.

17. Ibid., 5.

18. Ibid., 8.

19. Walter Wilson, ed., *The Selected Writings of W. E. B. Du Bois* (New York: New American Library, 1970), 52; emphasis added.

20. Derrida, *Monolingualism of the Other*, 69.

21. Ernest Gaines, *A Lesson before Dying* (New York: Vintage, 1997), 8.

22. Ibid., 8.

23. Ibid.,13.

24. Ibid., 55.

25. Ralph Ellison, *Invisible Man* (New York: Random House, 1947), 3.

26. Bakhtin, *The Dialogic Imagination*, 162.

27. H. Beecher Hicks Jr., *Images of the Black Preacher* (Valley Forge: Judson Press, 1977), 39.

28. Ibid.

4. The Sermon as Art

1. Walter J. Ong, *Orality and Literacy: The Technologizing of the Word* (New York: Routledge, 1988), 7.

2. *The Collected Poems of Langston Hughes,* edited by Arnold Rampersad and David Roessel (New York: Vintage, 1995), 51.

3. Elochukwu E. Uzukwu, *Worship as Body Language: An African Orientation* (Collegeville, Minn.: Liturgical Press, 1997), 3.

4. Albert J. Raboteau, *Canaan Land: A Religious History of African Americans* (Oxford: Oxford University Press, 2001), 45.

5. Ibid., 46.

6. Janheinz Jahn, *Muntu: An Outline of the New Culture* (New York: Grace Press, 1961), 164.

7. Ibid., 164.

8. Ibid.

9. Ibid.

10. Manuel Scott taught an evangelism class at the National Baptist Congress of Christian Education that usually had several thousand laity, preachers, and pastors in attendance. He is the author of the book *From a Black Brother* (Nashville: Broadman, 1971).

11. David James Randolph, *The Renewal of Preaching* (Philadelphia: Fortress Press, 1969), 99.

12. Miles Jerome Jones was Professor of Homiletics at the Samuel DeWitt Proctor School of Theology, Virginia Union University, Richmond, Virginia. He is author of *Preaching Papers* and coauthor with James H. Harris and Jerome C. Ross of *Proclamation 6: Interpreting the Lessons of the Church Year, Series B, Lent* (Minneapolis: Fortress Press, 1996).

13. See 1 Corinthians 2:4–5.

14. See my discussion of preaching as linguistic play in *Preaching Liberation* (Minneapolis: Fortress Press, 1995), 73–74.

15. Simon Blocker, *The Secret of Preaching Power* (Grand Rapids: Eerdmans, 1951), 137.

16. Ibid., 138.

17. Ibid., 139.

18. This language is used by hip-hop rapper Q-Tip. It is creative use of the English language and equivalent to "vibrant thing."

19. See Henry H. Mitchell, *Black Preaching* (New York: Harper and Row, 1979), and *The Recovery of Preaching* (San Francisco: Harper and Row, 1977).

20. Mitchell, *Black Preaching*, 188.

21. See Don M. Wardlaw, ed., *Preaching Biblically* (Philadelphia: Westminster, 1983), 21.

22. Thomas G. Long, *Preaching and the Literary Forms of the Bible* (Philadelphia: Fortress Press, 1989), 12–13.

23. Cleophus J. LaRue, *The Heart of Black Preaching* (Louisville: Westminster John Knox, 2000), 4.

24. John Malcus Ellison, *They Who Preach* (Nashville: Broadman, 1956), 104 (emphasis added).

25. See Steven Mailloux, "Interpretation," chap. 9 in *Critical Terms for Literary Study*, ed. Frank Lentrichia and Thomas McLaughlin (Chicago: University of Chicago Press, 1990), 122.

26. Ferdinand de Saussure, *Course in General Linguistics* (New York: McGraw-Hill, 1959), 10.

27. Friedrich Nietzsche, *Human, All Too Human* (Cambridge: Cambridge University Press, 1986), 99–100.

28. Jacques Derrida, *Monolingualism of the Other or the Prosthesis of Origin* (Stanford: Stanford University Press, 1998), 72.

29. Herbert Marcuse, *The Aesthetic Dimension: Toward a Critique of Marxist Aesthetics* (Boston: Beacon, 1978), 41.

5. The Sermon as Story

1. Fred B. Craddock, *Overhearing the Gospel* (Nashville: Abingdon, 1978), 16.

2. See Robert Alter, *The Art of Biblical Narrative* (New York: Basic, 1981), 34ff.

3. Hans W. Frei, *The Eclipse of Biblical Narrative: A Study of Eighteenth-and Nineteenth-Century Hermeneutics* (New Haven: Yale University Press, 1974), 15–16.

4. Miles Jerome Jones, a long-standing homiletics teacher and preacher, a handout on the expanded definitions of preaching, Virginia Union University, School of Theology, 2002.

5. See Alter, *Art of Biblical Narrative*, 34ff.

6. Ibid., 32–33.

7. Ernest Gaines, *A Lesson before Dying* (New York: Vintage, 1997), 217.

8. Ibid., 217–218.

9. See Walter Brueggemann, *Cadences of Home: Preaching among Exiles* (Louisville: Westminster John Knox, 1997), 26.

10. Ibid., 25.

11. Ibid., 30.

12. Brian K. Blount, *Then the Whisper Put On Flesh: New Testament Ethics in African American Context* (Nashville: Abingdon, 2001), 29.

13. Ibid., 40.

14. Ibid.

15. R. G. Coolingwood, *The Principles of Art* (London: Oxford University Press, 1958), 142.

16. Gordon D. Kaufman, *The Theological Imagination: Constructing the Concept of God* (Philadelphia: Westminster, 1981), 11.

17. James Engell, *The Creative Imagination: Enlightenment to Romanticism* (Cambridge, Mass.: Harvard University Press, 1981), 305.

18. James Weldon Johnson, *God's Trombones: Seven Negro Sermons in Verse* (New York: Viking, 1955), 5.

19. Ibid., 14.

20. Eugene Lowry, *The Sermon: Dancing on the Edge of Mystery* (Nashville: Abingdon, 1997), 23–24.

21. See ibid., 24.

22. Wayne Bradley Robinson, editor, *Journeys toward Narrative Preaching* (New York: Pilgrim, 1990), 4–5.

23. Jeffrey D. Arthurs, "Performing the Story: How to Preach First-Person Narrative Sermons," *Preaching* (March/April 1997): 30.

24. Ibid.

25. Eugene Lowry, *Sermon*, 24, 55–56.

26. Craddock, *Overhearing the Gospel*, 137.

27. William H. Willimon, "Preaching: Entertainment or Exposition?" *Christian Century,* February 28, 1992, 204–6.

28. Søren Kierkegaard, *Either/Or,* translated by David and Lillian Swenson, 2 vols. (Garden City: Anchor, 1959), 281.

29. Frei, *Eclipse of Biblical Narrative,* 27.

30. Ibid, 130.

31. Eugene Lowry, *The Homiletical Plot: The Sermon as Narrative Art Form* (Louisville: Westminster John Knox, 2001), 15–26.

32. Reinhold Niebuhr, *The Nature and Destiny of Man,* vol. 1 (New York: Scribners, 1941), 182.

33. Lowry, *Homiletical Plot,* 28–38.

34. David Larsen, *Telling the Old, Old Story: The Art of Narrative Preaching* (Grand Rapids: Kregel, 1995), 131–32. The author has relied heavily on the following sources to explicate narrative preaching: Eugene Lowry, *The Homiletical Plot* (Atlanta: John Knox, 1980); idem, *The Sermon: Dancing the Edge of Mystery* (Nashville: Abingdon, 1997); idem, *How to Preach a Parable* (Nashville: Abingdon, 1989); Richard Jensen, *Telling the Story: Variety and Imagination in Preaching* (Minneapolis: Augsburg, 1980); and David Larsen, *Telling the Old, Old Story: The Art of Narrative Preaching* (Wheaton, Ill.: Crossway, 1995).

6. Preaching Plainly: How to Put the Sermon Together— The Harris Method

1. Melva Wilson Costen, *African American Christian Worship* (Nashville: Abingdon, 1993), 104.

2. See, for example, David Buttrick's great book *Homiletic: Moves and Structure* (Philadelphia: Fortress Press, 1987). Buttrick discusses the concept of moves in part 1 of the book, utilizing four chapters to explain and describe this new language of moves instead of points. He states, "In speaking of 'moves,' we are deliberately changing terminology. For years, preachers have talked of making *points* in sermons. The word "point" is peculiar; it implies a rational, at-a-distance pointing at things, some kind of objectification. . . . Instead, we are going to speak of moves, of making moves in a *move*ment of language." He continues, "We must see what sermons are made of—namely a series of rhetorical units or moves. So we must study moves to see how they are shaped out of words and sentences and how, in turn, they form in the odd shared consciousness we call a 'congregation'" (23–24, emphasis in original).

3. Noam Chomsky, *Latin America: From Colonization to Globalization,* introduction by Heinz Dieterich (Melbourne, Australia: Ocean, 1999), 4.

4. Fred B. Craddock, *Luke,* Interpretation (Louisville: John Knox, 1990), 115.

Index